DANGEROUS DRUGS

VALIUM AND OTHER ANTIANXIETY DRUGS

CATHLEEN D. SMALL

Cavendish Square
New York

Published in 2016 by Cavendish Square Publishing, LLC
243 5th Avenue, Suite 136, New York, NY 10016

First Edition

Website: cavendishsq.com

This publication represents the opinions and views of the author based on his or her personal experience, knowledge, and research. The information in this book serves as a general guide only. The author and publisher have used their best efforts in preparing this book and disclaim liability rising directly or indirectly from the use and application of this book.

CPSIA Compliance Information: Batch #WS15CSQ

All websites were available and accurate when this book was sent to press.

Library of Congress Cataloging-in-Publication Data

Small, Cathleen.
Valium and other antianxiety drugs / Cathleen D. Small.
pages cm. — (Dangerous drugs)
Includes glossary.
Includes bibliographical references and index.
ISBN 978-1-50260-556-6 (hardcover) ISBN 978-1-50260-557-3 (ebook)
1. Benzodiazepine abuse. 2. Diazepan—Toxicology. 3. Benzodiazepines—Side effects.
4. Anxiety—Treatment—Complications. I. Title.

RC568.B45S63 2016
362.29'9—dc23

2014049269

Editorial Director: David McNamara
Editor: Fletcher Doyle
Copy Editor: Rebecca Rohan
Art Director: Jeffrey Talbot
Designer: Stephanie Flecha
Senior Production Manager: Jennifer Ryder-Talbot
Production Editor: Renni Johnson
Photo Research: J8 Media

The photographs in this book are used by permission and through the courtesy of: Paul Matthew Photography/Shutterstock.com, cover; Santi Visalli/Archive Photos/Getty Images, 4; BSIP/UIG/Getty Images, 7; Win McNamee/Getty Images, 8; John Greim/LightRocket/ Getty Images, 12; Joshya/Shutterstock.com, 16; BSIP/UIG/Getty images, 18; Mof/iStockphoto.com, 20; Leonello/iStock/Thinkstock, 22; Stephen Lovekin/Getty Images, 23; Roy Scott/Icon Images/Getty Images, 27; Sturti/E+/Getty Images, 29; Photographee.eu/ Shutterstock.com, 31; Rauluminate/iStock/Thinkstock, 34; Alainjuteau/iStockphoto.com, 36; Ethan Miller/Getty Images, 39; Doug Menuez/Photodisc/Getty Images, 42; MachineHeadz/iStockphoto.com, 44; Windzepher/iStock/Thinkstock, 47; Jonathan Wiggs/The Boston Globe/Getty Images, 48; Cultura Limited/Superstock, 51; Richard Clark/E+/Getty Images, 56; Ahturne/Shutterstock.com, 58.

Printed in the United States of America

Contents

CHAPTER ONE

Mother's Little Helper

ANXIETY IS A FEELING WE ALL KNOW. It might hit before an important test, before taking the stage in the spring musical, or when things aren't going well at home. For most of us, thankfully, it is a passing feeling. We get through the test, we finish our run in the school play, and the problems at home smooth out. But for some people, anxiety is more than that. For some people, the nervousness or unease is chronic, and every morning begins with a familiar, sinking feeling about what could go wrong or how we can make it through the day.

For these people, anxiety is often an actual disorder. There are many forms of anxiety disorder, including social anxiety (anxiety about social situations), **phobias** (intense

Leo Sternbach's research for Hoffmann-La Roche in the 1950s led to the creation of Valium.

fear of specific objects or situations), panic disorders (feelings of intense anxiety that strike with no warning and cause frightening physical symptoms, such as heart **palpitations**), and generalized anxiety.

For a person suffering from an anxiety disorder, medication can be the only answer, as the anxiety can be caused by an imbalance in brain chemistry. Over the years, scientists have developed two main classes of drugs to treat anxiety disorders: benzodiazepines and antidepressants.

Benzodiazepines

Benzodiazepines—or benzos, as they are sometimes known—got their name because they are chemically composed of a benzene ring and a diazepine ring. Commonly used benzos include Ativan, Dalmane, Doral, Halcion, Klonopin, Librium, Paxipam, ProSom, Restoril, Serax, Tranxene-SD, Valium, Versed, and Xanax. Of those, Ativan, Klonopin, Valium, and Xanax are the best known: they were among the one hundred most prescribed medications in the 1990s. Xanax is considered one of the most addictive drugs—some say it is more addictive than heroin.

Benzos were created in the 1950s. Librium, the first benzo, was created at Hoffmann-La Roche somewhat accidentally. A scientist named Leo Sternbach was working on developing tranquilizers, but he was disappointed in the initial results from his work. He moved on to another project, but two years later, in 1957, one of his co-workers, Earl Reeder, was cleaning

the lab and found a leftover **compound**, chlordiazepoxide, from Sternbach's research. Sternbach hadn't focused on that particular compound in his research, but when researchers used it in animal tests, they found it had strong effects as a **sedative**, **anticonvulsant**, and muscle relaxant. Buoyed by the successful results, Hoffmann-La Roche quickly introduced the compound as Librium. Three years later, in 1963, they followed that up with Valium, a similar benzo. The two drugs were wildly successful, especially as sedatives and for hypnotic uses. Doctors widely prescribed Valium to anyone feeling anxiety, and it was especially popular among women. Use of the drug was so common in Great Britain

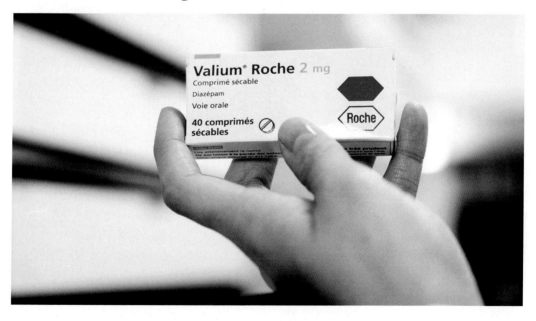

"Mother's Little Helper" took Great Britain by storm in the 1960s.

DEATH OF A MODEL

Vickie Lynn Hogan might've been just another woman quietly addicted to benzos—except that she spent her adult life in and out of the spotlight, first as a model for Guess Jeans and Lane Bryant, then as the twenty-six-year-old bride of eighty-nine-year-old billionaire oil tycoon J. Howard Marshall, and finally as the star of her own reality show. Better known as Anna Nicole Smith, she was frequently in the media as the family of her deceased husband—Marshall died thirteen months after their marriage—fought to keep his $1.6 billion estate out of her hands, insisting that the young model had married him only for his money.

Aside from the lawsuit, Smith stayed in the public eye due to her frequently odd behavior. She was known to be erratic and unpredictable, and many who knew her confirmed her addiction to prescription drugs. After her

Benzo addiction played a role in Anna Nicole Smith's death.

twenty-year-old son, Daniel, died of an overdose of prescription drugs Zoloft, Lexapro, and methadone in September 2006, Smith went into a downward spiral. She was found dead five months later of a drug overdose, leaving her infant daughter motherless. Toxicology tests run during the autopsy later showed she had four benzos in her system—Valium, Klonopin, Ativan, and Serax—along with the sedative chloral hydrate, the anticonvulsant Topamax, and Benadryl. All of these drugs were prescribed or over-the-counter; none were illegal substances. And yet, they were enough to take the life of a thirty-nine-year-old mother.

that the rock and roll band The Rolling Stones recorded a song about it in 1966. The song was titled "Mother's Little Helper."

When used as prescribed, benzodiazepines are relatively safe drugs with fairly few side effects. In fact, benzos became popular so quickly after their 1960 introduction because they were considered far safer than the **barbiturates** that had been used as sedatives and hypnotic drugs for years. It was relatively easy to overdose on barbiturates because they caused respiratory depression, but that danger was almost nonexistent with benzos. However, remember that nonexistent doesn't mean impossible—Edgar Rosenberg, the husband of famed comedienne Joan Rivers, committed suicide by taking a lethal dose of Valium in 1987. And people who mix benzos with alcohol are at greater risk of suffering a lethal overdose.

All drugs, prescription or otherwise, have side effects, and benzos are no exception. Common side effects include:

- **Psychomotor retardation**. This is a slowing of motor skills and reactions. For this reason, people taking benzos are warned not to drive or use heavy machinery.
- **Memory impairment**. This can be a positive or negative side effect. Because benzos can cause anterograde amnesia (that is, inability to recall recent past events), they are successfully used as a mild sedative for minor surgeries or medical procedures. However, amnesia is obviously not desirable when people are trying to go about the normal events of their day.
- **Paradoxical disinhibition**. Behavioral tendencies that are normally kept under wraps due to social restraints may become apparent. People can get more excitable, irritated, aggressive, hostile, and/ or impulsive. In rare cases, this has resulted in people going into a rage and attacking someone or something.
- **Depression**. A link between benzo use and depressive symptoms has been noted, and some people even begin to feel suicidal when using benzos.

- **Adverse effects in pregnancy**. Benzos are addictive and can cause a woman's unborn child to become addicted. The child will experience withdrawal symptoms when it is born or when the mother stops using benzos.
- **Tolerance**. People who use benzos for an extended period of time build up a tolerance to the benzos' effects and require greater doses of the drug to achieve the same result. This can lead to dependence.
- **Dependence**. Benzos are addictive. Just like any street drug, such as cocaine or heroin, benzos are habit-forming, and addicts go through physical and mental withdrawal symptoms when they finally stop using them. Interestingly, addicts are not often addicted only to benzos; the addiction normally goes hand in hand with dependence on alcohol, other prescribed drugs such as methadone, or illegal substances, such as heroin or cocaine. This is because benzos interact with these other substances in various ways—sometimes accentuating the highs and sometimes softening the lows.

A Safer Alternative?

Benzodiazepines were created for a positive reason: as a treatment for people suffering from anxiety or related conditions. The problem is that when used on a regular basis, benzos are addictive and lose their efficacy, meaning the

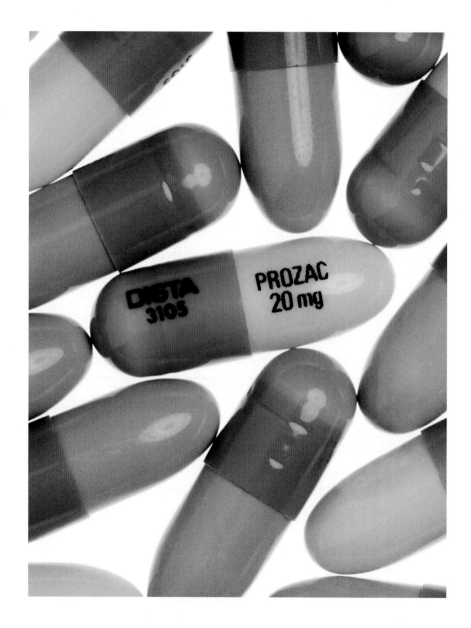

Prozac is considered a safer, non-habit-forming alternative to benzos.

person requires consistently higher doses. There are other options for the treatment of anxiety and related conditions. **Inhibitors** and tricyclic antidepressants, such as Prozac, Zoloft, Effexor, and Elavil, don't have the immediate effect of a benzo, but they are believed to be the best long-term treatments for people suffering from anxiety disorders, due to their relative safety and the fact that they are not typically habit-forming. In addition, anticonvulsants, **atypical neuroleptics**, **antihypertensives**, and the drug buspirone have shown promise in treating various types of anxiety, though antidepressants are typically the first course of non-benzo treatment.

Make no mistake, though: even antidepressants have side effects. They may not be physically addictive, like benzos, but they do come with a range of side effects, including:

- Nausea
- Weight gain and increased appetite
- Fatigue
- Insomnia
- Dry mouth
- Blurred vision
- Dizziness
- Anxiety

The fact that you can get anxiety from taking a drug to relieve anxiety is a paradox. The truth is that drugs don't work the same in every person—other medications you're taking or other aspects of your body chemistry can alter how they work. So it's important to pay attention to how a particular medication is working for you and talk to your doctor about adjusting it if necessary.

The potential side effects from antidepressants aren't particularly pleasant-sounding, but note that "dependence" isn't listed among them. That's because people are very unlikely to become physically dependent on antidepressants. However, that doesn't mean antidepressants aren't habit-forming from a psychological standpoint. With any drug, it's important to recognize how easy it is to start believing you need the drug to function. Your body may not physically need the drug, but your mind may tell you it does. Still, a mental dependence on a drug is, in theory, a lot easier to break than a physical one. For that reason antidepressants are generally considered safer than benzos.

CHAPTER TWO

The Benzo Allure

BEFORE YOU CAN UNDERSTAND THE dangers of addiction, you need to understand how a particular substance works in your body—and why you'd even want to have it in your body.

Benzodiazepines, such as Valium and Xanax, are considered central nervous system depressants. They work to slow the nervous system. They affect everything from emotional reactions, memory, thinking, and consciousness to **muscle tone** and coordination.

The nervous system is composed of neurons, which are individual nerve cells. Nerve signals travel through a neuron and are transported to the next neuron using chemicals called **neurotransmitters**. The spaces between the neurons are called **synapses**, and the neurotransmitters float in these synapses.

There are two common neurotransmitters in the brain. One is glutamate, and it increases the number of nerve signals that pass between neurons. The other is gamma-aminobutyric acid, an amino acid called GABA. It reduces the number of nerve signals that pass between neurons, so it slows or calms the body. The brain's synapses have GABA receptors. The benzos make GABA receptors work better. When GABA binds to these receptors, it opens channels in neurons that allow ions to enter. When the receptors work better, more ions get in. These ions control fear and anxiety by calming the neurons that are overexcited.

Alcohol works the same way on neurotransmitters. This is why it's particularly dangerous to use alcohol and benzos at the same time: their added effect can slow the body too much.

Synapse

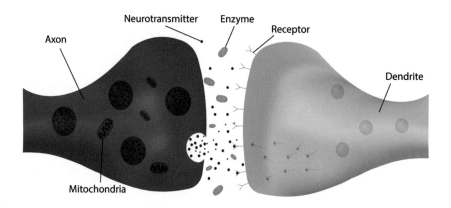

Neurotransmitters relay signals from one neuron, across a synapse, to receptors on a target neuron. Mitochondria generate chemical energy. Dendrites move signals to the body of the neuron.

At common low doses, benzos are useful as sedatives, antianxiety drugs, insomnia treatments, anticonvulsants for people prone to seizures, and muscle relaxants, specifically because they quiet the overactive brain chemicals and thus calm the body. And at higher doses, benzos are useful as sedatives for certain medical procedures because they can put the body into a very relaxed state. A patient who is given a benzodiazepine prior to a medical procedure won't go to sleep as a fully sedated patient would; rather, he or she would be in an altered, calm state. For that reason, an anesthesiologist wouldn't use benzos on a patient before a major surgery, but for a relatively minor but anxiety-producing procedure, such as a colonoscopy or a root canal, benzos can be a good solution.

Three Forms of Benzodiazepines

Benzodiazepines come in short-, intermediate-, or long-acting varieties. Short-acting benzos take effect quickly, whereas long-acting benzos do not usually have an immediate effect. For something like insomnia, where instant relief is desired, short- and intermediate-acting benzos are preferred, although they tend not to be effective if used on an everyday basis. For a longer-term issue that requires more consistent medicating, such as general anxiety disorder, long-acting benzos are a better choice.

Xanax and Klonopin both have rapid onsets, for example, but the effects of Xanax last for only a few hours, whereas the effects of Klonopin can last for several days. This is

WOMEN'S ISSUE

Early marketing campaigns for antianxiety drugs were primarily aimed at women. One advertisement from the 1960s spoke of "A Whole New World ... of Anxiety." It stressed the new challenges the modern woman was facing, such as heading off to college. The advertising worked: by 1974 there were nearly sixty million prescriptions filled for Valium, and a majority of the customers were women.

The National Institute of Health reports that "Women have consistently higher prevalence rates of anxiety disorders" than men. And, they are "not only more prevalent but also more disabling in women than in men."

Women's use of antianxiety medications increased by 29 percent from 2001 to 2011, and they were twice as likely to use such drugs as men.

There are several possible reasons for the disparity in drug use. Dr. David Muzina, a psychiatrist, said women are much more likely to seek treatment than men for psychological issues. He also said that Valium and other antianxiety drugs act right away so they are good at helping people adjust to changes in their lives on a short-term basis.

These changes include problems in a relationship or loss of a job. Another explanation is that working mothers deal with more things that cause emotional stress than men do.

The World Health Organization (WHO) says there is a gender bias in the diagnosis of mental health disorders. It also reported that doctors are more likely to prescribe mood-altering drugs to women. The WHO also said that mental health problems are more persistent in women, and called for more research into the reasons why.

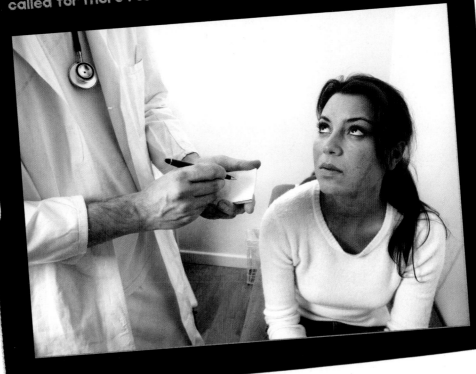

The majority of prescriptions for benzodiazepines are written for women.

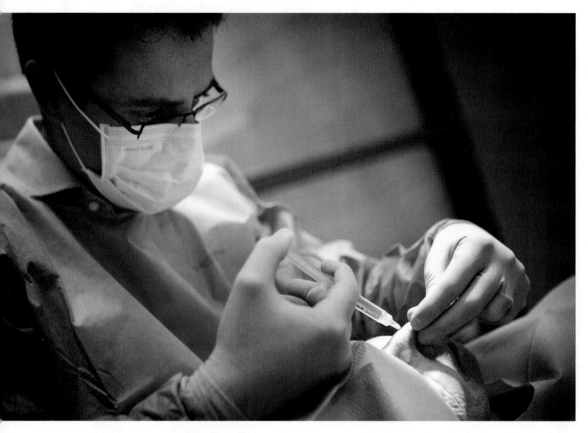

Short-acting benzodiazepines are often used as "conscious sedation" during minor medical procedures, such as dermatologic surgeries.

determined by how the drug breaks down in the body and its **half-life**, or the time it takes for the concentration of the drug in the body to decrease by half. Valium and Klonopin are probably the best-known long-acting benzos. Well-known medium-acting benzos include Librium, Xanax, Ativan, and Rohypnol. Short-acting benzos include Versed and Halcion.

When Librium was introduced, with Valium following a few years later, the drugs were marketed as being safe alternatives to barbiturates. Like benzos, barbiturates are central nervous system depressants, and like benzos, they are psychologically and physically addictive. Barbiturates are derived from barbituric acid, which was first synthesized in 1864. Its medical efficacy, however, wasn't known until 1903, when two German scientists discovered it was useful in euthanizing, or killing humanely, dogs. After that, it was used for sedatives and "sleeping pills" for many years, and only in the 1950s did its addictive qualities and its effect on behavior become known.

Overdose by barbiturates isn't unusual because they can be toxic at surprisingly low doses. Among the many lives claimed by barbiturate overdoses are actresses Marilyn Monroe and Judy Garland and rock legend Jimi Hendrix. Given the ease with which one can overdose on barbiturates, perhaps it's not surprising that they are prescribed for assisted suicide in states where that act is legal.

Barbiturates are still prescribed for patients suffering from migraines or epileptic seizures, and they are sometimes used for general anesthesia. However, these uses are strictly monitored by the prescribing physician so that patients don't become addicted or inadvertently overdose.

Given the dangers of barbiturates, it's easy to see how benzos were considered to be miracle drugs. They worked on the same issues as barbiturates—anxiety, insomnia,

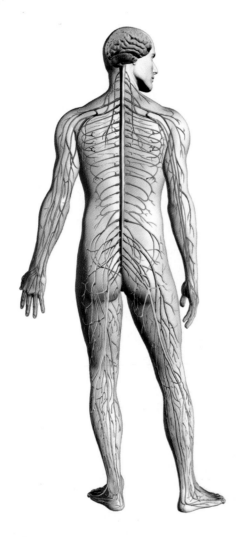

Benzodiazepines act as central nervous system depressants—they slow down the nervous system.

seizures—but theoretically without the dangerous side effects of addiction and possible overdose. They were so popular that in 1975, there were 103 million prescriptions issued for them in the United States alone. And in the early 1980s, thirty-two million prescriptions for benzos were written in Britain—at a time when the country's entire population wasn't quite sixty million.

While it's true that people are much less likely to overdose on benzos than on barbiturates, doctors and scientists eventually discovered that like barbiturates, benzos were in fact physically and psychologically addictive. Overdose is also still possible—even if it's not as easy as with barbiturates. Most overdoses from benzos occur when the person combines benzos with alcohol or other prescription drugs. Anna Nicole Smith is one example, but other celebrities who have overdosed on benzos in combination with other substances include singer Amy Winehouse, actress Brittany

22

Murphy, actor Heath Ledger, and disc jockey DJ AM (born Adam Goldstein). Singer Whitney Houston also had benzos in her system when she died from a drug overdose in 2012.

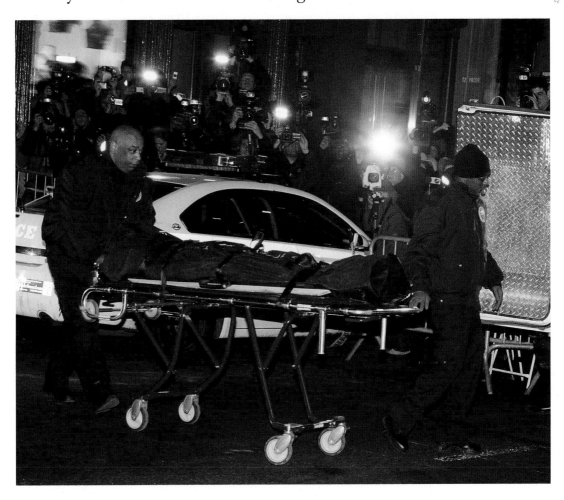

The body of actor Heath Ledger is removed from his New York City apartment on January 22, 2008. Benzos were among the substances found in Ledger's bloodstream during his autopsy.

When benzos are used correctly and safely, they have some positive effects. For anxiety disorders, benzos are extremely effective—more so than barbiturates and **antipsychotic** medicines. For a person who suffers from panic attacks during, say, her twice-yearly dental cleaning, Valium or Xanax can be a godsend—the dangerous side effects are relatively few, and these drugs provide excellent short-term relief during panic-inducing situations.

For people suffering from **epilepsy**, benzos can also be beneficial. Some anticonvulsants have unpleasant side effects, and benzos can provide significant improvement from seizures. In fact, Valium is sometimes used as a treatment during a seizure, and it has been shown to reduce the possibility of death due to the seizure.

Benzos can also be useful as a treatment for withdrawal from alcohol or other substances. Along with withdrawal symptoms can come delirium, seizures, and high fever—benzos have shown effectiveness in treating all of these. It is rather ironic, though, that benzos are sometimes used to treat withdrawal symptoms when they themselves can result in withdrawal symptoms.

Valium and other benzos have some useful purposes and they were created for a positive end. However, when misused, these drugs can have very negative effects.

CHAPTER THREE

Mind and Body

FIFTY YEARS OF USE AND RESEARCH HAVE shown that Valium and other benzodiazepines have a number of negative effects on health and **cognition**, along with the risk of addiction. Cognition refers to conscious mental activities, such as thinking, understanding, learning, and remembering.

There is still disagreement among researchers about the side effects of these drugs. Some feel that long-term use of Valium or other benzos could impair **visual-spatial** ability, the speed at which you process information, and verbal learning. Others argue that in people who use benzos, these deficits could be present because of their underlying anxiety or depression—both conditions are known to affect cognition, too. In an attempt to sort out the cause of cognitive deficits, in 2005 researchers analyzed the available data from studies of patients who had been treated with benzos on a long-term basis. The researchers concluded that cognitive impairment did occur in these patients, and that their condition improved when they stopped using benzos. However, even after the patients in the studies stopped using benzos, their cognitive function didn't return to the levels of control participants in the studies who had never taken benzos. These results prompted researchers to advise that patients should be informed of possible cognitive effects resulting from the long-term use of benzos.

As early as 1976, when about one hundred million prescriptions for benzos were being written in the United States annually, Dr. David Knott from the University of Tennessee expressed concern about the possibility that benzos caused short-term memory loss and damage to the brain's cerebral cortex. He wondered whether that damage would turn out to be permanent. And in 1982, Malcolm Lader, a British professor of **psychopharmacology**, voiced similar concerns when he reported that brain scans showed that a small group of patients who had been taking Valium for several years showed evidence of brain damage.

The evidence to support the theory that long-term benzo use may cause damage to the brain continued to mount over the years. Anxiety specialist Isaac Marks published his concerns in a 1989 issue of the *Archives of General Psychiatry*.

He felt the long-term side effects of Xanax observed in long-term users had been minimized or ignored. These side effects include sedation, uncoordinated movement, and fatigue thought to be due to damage to the brain.

PERSONALITY CHANGES

Negative psychological effects have also been noted in longtime benzo users. Award-winning science writer and Pulitzer Prize finalist Robert Whitaker pointed out in his 2010 book *Anatomy of an Epidemic: Magic Bullets, Psychiatric Drugs, and the Astonishing Rise of Mental Illness in America* that as far back as 1983, the World Health Organization noted deteriorated

More than fifty years of research have led to the conclusion that long-term use of benzos has a negative effect on cognition.

personal care and social interactions in longtime users of benzos. He also revealed that a 2007 French study of more than four thousand longtime benzo users found that a majority had "major depressive episodes and generalized anxiety disorder." And a 2007 study of more than 5,500 patients in the United States also indicated that those at risk for depression had a higher risk of developing depression when treated with benzos.

In addition to depression and anxiety, other psychological effects may include clouded thinking, irritability, memory impairment, aggression, personality changes, **disinhibition**, mood swings, and social deterioration. In 1998, Dr. Peter R. Breggin of the Center for the Study of Psychiatry and Psychology published a paper in *The Journal of Mind and Behavior* that said that short-acting benzos, such as Xanax and Halcion, were "especially prone to cause psychological and behavioral abnormalities" and that such effects could wreak havoc in the lives of benzo users and their families. On a support forum for benzo users, participants had this to say about behavioral abnormalities and personality changes:

- "While on [benzos], I had a really hard time taking the initiative to do *anything*."
- "Clonazepam made me apathetic, pessimistic, paranoid, and depressed. It took away my motivation and ambition and robbed me of my creativity."
- "Anger, often for no good reason. Anti-social. *Very* anxious and depressed. Tired and lazy. Racing thoughts."
- "All my emotions are far more uncontrollable, extreme and exaggerated. There is a callousness about me now."

Many benzo users report feeling **apathy**—they feel indifferent about things that should bring them joy or sadness. They have little interest in things that used to bring them

Use of benzodiazepines has been found to cause personality changes, such as apathy, depression, and laziness.

pleasure. However, some benzo users don't recognize these personality or behavioral changes as being due to benzo use—they attribute them to being part of their mental illness instead. In reference to this trend, Dr. Breggin coined the term "medical spellbinding," which is basically a mind-numbing in which people on psychiatric medications, such as benzos, lose their self-awareness and become unable to make good choices about their own mental health. Instead of recognizing the possibility that medications may be responsible for effects on their behavior, they attribute the behavior to their own mental illness or sometimes blame it on external factors.

Physical Effects of Long-Term Benzo Use

Psychological effects are not the only type of negative effect from long-term benzo use. Reported physical effects of long-term benzo use include nausea, headaches, dizziness, tremors, loss of bladder control, lethargy, and insomnia and sleep impairment. Insomnia can be a vicious cycle. People may start taking benzos in part because they suffer from insomnia—a drug that lessens anxiety seems like a reasonable solution when someone can't relax enough to sleep. However, studies have shown that benzo use can in fact worsen insomnia—a study published in 2004 in the *Journal of Psychiatric Research* showed that chronic benzo use appeared to be associated with poor sleep quality. Heath Ledger, who died of an overdose of prescription drugs shortly after playing the Joker in *The Dark Knight*, told reporters

that he slept an average of only two hours each night during filming and that prescription drugs did not help.

Long-term benzo use changes a person's sleep architecture, mainly by causing a shortened time in deep and REM (rapid eye movement) sleep and an increased time in intermediate sleep. REM and deep sleep are critical factors to the quality of a person's sleep; decreasing the time a person spends in these states results in poor-quality sleep.

Addiction is the most dangerous effect of long-term benzo use. And in fact, a person doesn't have to use benzos for long to develop a habit. Some are more potent and habit-

Benzodiazepine use can cause negative changes in sleep patterns, resulting in insomnia and poor-quality sleep.

THE DEMONS OF WITHDRAWAL

Withdrawal may be one of the most difficult parts of dealing with a drug addiction. For example, Xanax, a popular and widely prescribed benzo, is known for having particularly nasty withdrawal symptoms, despite supposedly being a "mild" drug. Addiction specialist Dr. Jerry Callaway, who considers Xanax one of the most dangerous drugs he handles, reports that he finds it easier to help people get off of heroin than Xanax. "I'd rather take one hundred people off heroin than one person off Xanax because I know they'll have a year of withdrawal," he says.

Physical and psychological effects of withdrawal are very real and can range from mild to quite severe. With some drugs, withdrawal can have such serious side effects that the person needs to be hospitalized while undergoing the physical side effects of withdrawal. But even if the person going through withdrawal doesn't suffer from serious physical effects such as seizures or hallucinations, the side effects of insomnia, agitation, and anxiety alone can be overwhelming, causing many people to cave in to the pressure and take a benzo or other substance to "take the edge off."

forming than others—the illegal benzo Rohypnol is quite potent and highly addictive—but even the milder benzos, such as Valium, can quickly become addictive.

Some of the most difficult side effects occur when longtime benzo users try to discontinue use of the drugs. In 1990, the American Psychiatric Association Task Force grouped withdrawal symptoms from benzos into three groups—very frequent, common but less frequent, and uncommon.

Withdrawal Symptoms of Benzodiazepine Users

Very Frequent	Common but Less Frequent	Uncommon
Anxiety	Depression	Psychosis
Insomnia		Seizures
Restlessness		Persistent tinnitus (ringing of the ears)
Agitation		Confusion
Irritability		Paranoid delusions
Muscle tension		Hallucinations

The task force noted that these withdrawal symptoms could last for several weeks or even months, and that benzos with a shorter half-life tended to produce more intense symptoms.

Dangers to Older Users

A recent large-scale Canadian study of 1,796 Alzheimer's patients showed those who had used benzos for three months or more showed a 51 percent increase in their risk of developing **Alzheimer's disease**. The study, published in

A Canadian study showed that long-term use of benzos can lead to an increased risk for Alzheimer's disease.

the *British Medical Journal,* noted that the longer people were exposed to benzos, the greater their risk of developing Alzheimer's. In addition, the study showed that long-acting benzos, such as Valium, increased people's risk more than short-acting benzos, such as Xanax.

In the United States, in 2012, the American Geriatrics Society added benzos to the list of inappropriate drugs for older adults. Some of the side effects (such as confusion and cognitive difficulty) can result in elderly people falling and fracturing their bones, which tend to be more brittle than those of younger people, or having difficulty driving, resulting in auto accidents. However, according to professors at UC San Francisco and the Indiana University Center for Aging Research, despite the American Geriatrics Society's warning, nearly 50 percent of older adults continue to use benzos. This is because anxiety, insomnia, and depression are relatively common in elderly populations, and benzos have long been treatments for those conditions.

However you look at it, long-term use of benzos is dangerous. Addiction is a very real concern, but even if you're one of the lucky people who doesn't get physically addicted to the medication, there are many undesirable psychological and physical side effects. And as you get older, those concerns are heightened.

CHAPTER FOUR

Loss of Control

THE PHYSICAL AND PSYCHOLOGICAL effects of benzodiazepine addiction are numerous and concerning, but the social effects are far-reaching, too. An addiction to benzos doesn't just affect the addict; it affects everyone around him or her. Because these drugs are legitimately prescribed, it can sometimes be difficult to pinpoint them as a problem. However, benzos can indeed affect a person's behavior and cause real problems for the addict and for those around him or her.

Valium has been cited as the cause for aggressive outbursts and violence in some cases—in one particular case, a woman was acquitted of stabbing her husband to death when a professor provided medical testimony indicating that the woman's use of excessive Valium in the twelve hours before the stabbing had likely caused the violent outburst. The British National Formulary has suggested that benzos may produce "aggressive and **antisocial** acts." The link between benzos and crime is growing; a pilot study in one part of Scotland showed that 34 percent of persons arrested for crimes tested positive for benzos, and prisons in the US, Canada, Australia, and the UK have reported higher levels of aggression and violent acts among inmates who have been prescribed benzos. Instances of child, spousal, and elder abuse have also been attributed to benzo use, thought to be a result of a lack of normal inhibitions that control behavior.

Lack of inhibitions can be a real problem among benzo users. Rohypnol, a particularly potent benzo that is illegal in the United States, is known as the "date-rape drug" in part because people who take

Benzo use can lead to loss of inhibition, which can put users into potentially dangerous situations.

Rock star Stevie Nicks was prescribed Klonopin to combat a cocaine addiction. She then spent eight years fighting a benzo addiction.

it have lowered inhibitions and may engage in risky or **promiscuous** behavior. But Rohypnol is not the only such drug to contribute to promiscuous behavior—benzos in general are thought to lower inhibitions that would normally prevent a person from behaving promiscuously.

Every benzo user does not experience hostile behavior and lack of inhibitions. The drug affects people differently. Because benzos act on brain chemicals and electrical activity in the brain, it is difficult to predict how any person will react to them—the brain is too complex for this type of prediction to be 100 percent accurate. Neurosurgeon Frank Vertosick, Jr., author of *When the Air Hits Your Brain: Parables of Neurosurgery*, describes the brain as "a trillion nerve cells storing electrical patterns more numerous than the water molecules of the world's oceans." When you consider brain activity on that vast of a scale, it's understandable that we can't really know exactly how each person will react to a particular benzo.

Another effect that benzos can have on a person's social behavior is that they can put the person into a dull haze. Rock star Stevie Nicks, of Fleetwood Mac fame and later a successful solo artist, has experienced this firsthand, saying that Klonopin, a widely used benzo, made her a "zombie." In fact, she blames the drug for the fact that she never had a family. In the years when she would've likely had children, she was suffering through a Klonopin addiction that started when a psychiatrist at the Betty Ford Clinic prescribed her benzos to combat her cocaine addiction. She was first given

Valium, then Xanax, and ultimately Klonopin. She spent eight years of her life in the grips of Klonopin addiction, which she only successfully beat after a forty-five-day inpatient rehab stint that she claims felt like "somebody [opening] up a door and [pushing her] into hell."

Nicks isn't alone in being prescribed Klonopin by a well-meaning doctor. It's often used to prevent seizures and control withdrawal from other drugs. And while it's very successful at doing those things, it has the hidden danger of being very addictive by itself.

Hidden Dangers

Addiction itself is dangerous: the more you take benzos, the more your perceptions and actions are altered, which may cause you to make poor decisions. One of the scariest things about benzos is that people who take them often report feeling completely normal—even when their actions suggest otherwise. Thus, a person who is under the influence of a benzo may feel perfectly fine and able to get behind the wheel of a car, but in reality may be unable to safely operate a vehicle. This can be dangerous in any number of situations: benzos have a way of making people feel relaxed and in control even when they're not, which can lead to some very poor and even dangerous decisions and behaviors.

Another hidden danger is how benzos react with alcohol. Many prescription drugs have a "do not take with alcohol" warning on the bottle—this warning is so ubiquitous that

40

Benzos can make people lose control. When combined with alcohol, another central nervous system depressant, they can be lethal.

Benzos are not illegal substances; however, selling or supplying benzos to a person without a prescription is a criminal activity.

people tend to ignore it and assume the drug manufacturer is just being overly cautious. However, alcohol and benzos really do not mix well. Or rather, they mix too well. Both alcohol and benzos are central nervous system depressants that increase sedation, so if you take benzos and drink alcohol, it's essentially like taking a double—or more!—dose of benzos, and that can be dangerous or even deadly.

Although it is rare to overdose solely on benzos, it's not at all uncommon for a combination of benzos and alcohol or other drugs to result in an overdose, which can lead to death. Such was the case for model and actress Margaux Hemingway, granddaughter of Nobel Prize–winning author Ernest Hemingway, who committed suicide in 1996 by combining benzos and barbiturates. Only a few weeks later, an acclaimed Hollywood producer, Don Simpson, died from an unintentional overdose of benzos combined with other substances. And in the last several years, soldiers returning from the Middle East with **post-traumatic stress disorder** (PTSD) have died in their sleep after ingesting Klonopin, Paxil (a nonaddictive antidepressant), and Seroquel (an antipsychotic drug that is often prescribed for PTSD).

CRIME AND PUNISHMENT

Unlike an addiction to an illegal substance, such as cocaine or heroin, an addiction to benzos doesn't always have legal implications. Because many doctors are willing to write prescriptions for benzos, it's not overly difficult to get them. However, as an addiction grows and the person develops

COST OF A BENZO HABIT

It's difficult to quantify the cost of a benzo habit. Because benzos are legal, people usually get them by prescription, which is covered by insurance. However, certain benzos are offered on the street, and the cost depends on the drug. Valium is the best-known benzo and thus commands a relatively steep street price of around $3 to $5 per 10 mg pill. That doesn't sound like much until you realize that addicts frequently take more than one pill per day.

Rohypnol, which must be imported since it's not legally manufactured in the United States, is surprisingly less expensive than Valium. Sources describe the drug as "dirt cheap," at roughly $1 per pill.

a tolerance to the drug and needs more and more of it to achieve the desired effect, addicts often have to resort to illegal or unethical methods to maintain their supply of the drug. Ethical doctors will not continue to increase a person's prescription for a benzo, as that is a telltale sign of an addiction and can be quite dangerous. Addicts may then find multiple doctors to supply prescriptions (unbeknownst to each other), or they may forge prescriptions, or buy benzos on the street.

Depending on the state you live in and the offense, illegal possession or sale of benzodiazepines can result in jail time and/or a fine.

Possession, Sales, and Doing Time

Although in general it's not illegal to possess benzos, even if you don't have a prescription, it is illegal to supply them. Supplying benzos can result in a prison sentence of up to five years and/or an unlimited fine. So if you have a prescription for benzos, do not, under any circumstances, share them with anyone—if you do, you could be considered a supplier. And if you're getting benzos from someone other than your doctor, keep in mind that the person could be imprisoned for illegally supplying you with benzos.

Benzos that are not legal to have include nitrazepam and bromazepam (which have several trade names but are not marketed in the United States); Rohypnol, which isn't legally manufactured or marketed in the United States; and Restoril. Possessing one of these can result in a prison term and/or an unlimited fine.

It is also illegal in certain states, such as California, to possess drugs that were obtained by a forged prescription.

Forging a prescription is illegal and can be either a misdemeanor or a felony. The consequences vary from state to state, but in general, if you forge or alter a prescription, you can be found guilty of forgery and sentenced to jail time or a fine. If you are charged with a felony for the offense, your punishment will be much stiffer than if the charge is classified as a misdemeanor. How you are charged depends on the state the offense occurs in, your criminal history, and other situational factors. There's no one answer to how a person will be charged, but keep in mind that illegal possession or use of benzos is often considered a felony offense.

It's important to note that in the United States, benzos are classified by the federal Controlled Substances Act as Schedule IV drugs, meaning that the drugs are accepted for medical use but that they are addictive substances that can be abused.

CHAPTER FIVE

Getting Help

IF YOU OR SOMEONE YOU KNOW IS addicted to Valium or another antianxiety drug, it's important to safely get you or them weaned off of the drug. Stopping the use of any medication cold turkey, without warning, can have dangerous effects. Because of the addictive nature of these drugs, withdrawal symptoms can be intensified if the drug is abruptly stopped. It is important that the addicted person is monitored by a doctor and/or a drug counselor.

If you suspect a friend is addicted to Valium or other anxiety-reducing drugs, here are a few tips on helping your friend. First, speak up, because the sooner treatment starts the better it will be for them. Be prepared for their denials, but if you have facts to back up your suspicions you may get them into treatment. Don't be judgmental. Take care of yourself by

A drug addict going through withdrawal needs support during the time of struggle.

staying out of dangerous situations and don't blame yourself if the addict refuses to change his or her behavior. Most of all, if the addict is young, alert his or her parents.

Here are some other tips on what not to do, taken from the National Clearinghouse for Alcohol and Drug Information: Don't threaten addicts with punishment. Don't try to shame them, which could add to their drug dependency. Don't make excuses for them or cover their responsibilities so their behavior can be hidden. Don't hide or throw out their drugs, argue with them when they are high, or do drugs with them.

Doctors can provide a schedule under which the addicted person slowly decreases his or her drug use to wean off of the substance. And drug counselors can provide a supportive environment for the person struggling to adjust to life without the effects of a drug he or she has become dependent on to function. Addicts need to learn how to make decisions without the influence of drugs, and that can be challenging.

When it comes to conquering any sort of addiction—to illegal drugs, prescription drugs, or alcohol, for example—the options can be roughly divided into two groups:

- Inpatient rehabilitation
- Outpatient rehabilitation

Inpatient Rehabilitation

Inpatient rehabilitation centers and programs provide addicts with a place to stay while overcoming their addiction. The

50

environment is supervised twenty-four hours a day, seven days a week, so there is constant support available. The website Recovery.org states that patients with a mild to moderate benzo addiction may require a stay as short as twenty-eight days; however, the length of the stay depends completely on the individual and the strength of his or her addiction.

Sometimes inpatient recovery centers have private rooms, but often patients have a roommate, which can be beneficial to the recovery process. Group and individual therapy sessions are typically part of an inpatient recovery program, as well as programs and events designed to keep recovering addicts comfortable as they learn to live life drug-free.

The **detoxification** process at an inpatient recovery program is monitored and may be in the form of a tapered schedule that allows the addict to wean slowly off the

Inpatient and outpatient rehabilitation options exist for people addicted to benzos.

Symptoms of Benzo Abuse

Before a person can get help for benzo abuse, someone needs to recognize the problem.

If you suspect someone you know may be addicted to benzos, consider whether the person shows the following signs of abuse:

- Drowsiness
- Memory problems
- Dizziness
- Weakness
- Nausea or vomiting
- Dilated eyes
- Reports of blurred or double vision
- Impaired driving and slow reaction time

Potentially more serious but less frequent signs of abuse include:

- Confusion
- Hallucinations

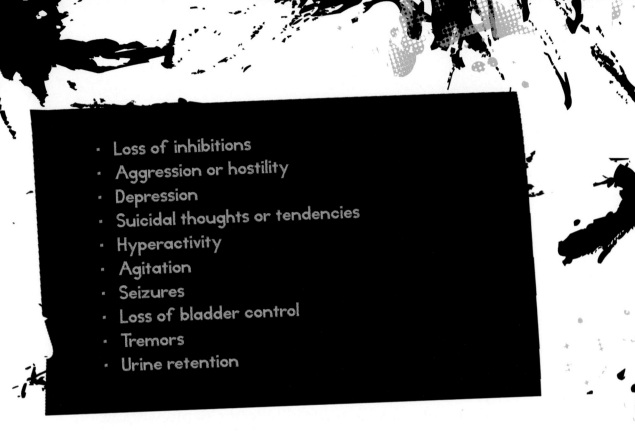

- Loss of inhibitions
- Aggression or hostility
- Depression
- Suicidal thoughts or tendencies
- Hyperactivity
- Agitation
- Seizures
- Loss of bladder control
- Tremors
- Urine retention

drug, or it may be a medically assisted cold turkey method. Either way, the person suffering from addiction to benzos is carefully monitored and continually assessed to ensure a successful detoxification.

After recovering benzo addicts are released from an inpatient recovery center, they may choose to go back to their previous living arrangements, or they may choose to spend some time in a halfway house, where they live with other recovering addicts but can go to work and participate in social activities.

Outpatient Rehabilitation

Outpatient rehabilitation from an addiction to benzos isn't as simple as checking in with a doctor once a week to monitor the detoxification process. Recovering from a benzo addiction is a serious and sometimes dangerous process. People addicted to Valium and other benzos can experience anything from weakness and vomiting to hallucinations, seizures, and suicidal thoughts. People choosing to conquer a benzo addiction through outpatient rehabilitation require close monitoring by a professional.

Outpatient rehabilitation includes careful monitoring of an addict's physical and mental state, but it also requires education. A comprehensive outpatient program generally includes discussions, therapy groups, lectures, homework assignments, and individual therapy sessions to help person learn about the dangers of his or her addiction and coping strategies for adjusting to life in the world without the influence of benzos.

Exercise, meditation, nutrition, and healthy sleep are also usually components of a successful outpatient recovery program. Addicts have to learn how to live a healthy overall lifestyle to rebuild their self-confidence and withstand the temptation to relapse into old habits.

Finding the Best Option

The treatment program that will work best for someone addicted to benzos depends on many factors, including the person's support system, level of addiction, resources, and past experiences with rehabilitation.

Outpatient treatment programs require addicts to be more accountable for their behavior. In an outpatient program,

54

addicts don't have constant supervision to ensure that they don't relapse. This is where support systems and past experiences factor in. If addicts have tried to kick a benzo habit through an outpatient program before and have relapsed, they may need a more intensive inpatient program where someone else holds them accountable for what they ingest. Similarly, if addicts don't have a strong support system of family and/or friends to help them when they are tempted to start using benzos again, outpatient recovery can be very difficult. Make no mistake: kicking any addiction is difficult, and even the strongest of people need help sometimes. If the support system isn't there, then the person may be better off in an inpatient rehabilitation program.

Level of addiction plays a role here, too, simply because the greater the addiction to benzos, the more difficult physical and psychological withdrawal will be. The physical symptoms of withdrawal can be crippling and dangerous, so if a person is heavily dependent on benzos, it is probably best to seek treatment in an inpatient facility where the physical symptoms of withdrawal can be closely monitored.

Psychological withdrawal can be just as difficult as physical withdrawal, and certainly longer lasting. Imagine having lived months or years of your life in the haze of addiction to antianxiety drugs. You've made all of your decisions and faced a range of situations with the help of drugs to calm you down. Now imagine having to face those same types of decisions and situations without something to help you feel calm. The prospect is daunting, and it can take addicts a

Therapy sessions are an important part of any drug addiction treatment program.

long time to feel comfortable in a world that is not clouded by the haze of benzos and antianxiety medications.

As helpful as inpatient rehabilitation sounds, though, it is not always feasible. Some people don't have the financial resources to pay for inpatient treatment, which can be extremely expensive. The Hazelden Betty Ford Foundation, which offers inpatient and outpatient treatment options in several US locations, estimates that outpatient treatment typically costs about $10,000, whereas the four- to six-week inpatient treatment programs typically run from $20,000 to $32,000. Insurance can help with the costs, and there are sometimes financial-assistance programs available, but the bottom line is that treatment for drug addiction is expensive, and it's even more so if that treatment is on an inpatient basis.

Know Your Options

The best way to handle an addiction to benzos is never to form an addiction in the first place. The problem is, you may start taking benzos with the best of intentions—just as a temporary way to handle anxiety or insomnia or some related condition. But addiction sneaks up on you—in a very short time you may feel unable to cope without the help of benzos. You may not feel like an addict, but if you can't imagine living long term without the help of benzos, you're on the threshold of addiction, and it's a quick fall off the cliff from there.

Being able to stop using the drug for short periods of time doesn't mean you don't have a problem. Addicts are notorious for being able to stop whatever substance they're addicted to for days, weeks, or even months and then proclaiming, "See? I don't have a problem! If I did, I wouldn't be able to stop!" But if you go back to the drug after temporarily stopping, it may indicate an addiction.

If you have anxiety or a related disorder that you cannot manage without the help of prescription drugs, be aware of your options. Talk to your doctor about trying nonaddictive antidepressants or other non-habit-forming drugs, rather than benzos. And if you absolutely must, for some reason, use benzos, be very familiar with the warning signs of addiction and work closely with your doctor to ensure that you don't fall into an addictive pattern.

More than anything, seek help. If you feel stressed, anxious, or alone, talk to someone about it. If you don't feel

comfortable talking to your parents, consider talking to a trusted teacher, a counselor, or even a friend's parents. And get involved with activities that surround you with people who make you feel comfortable. Adolescence can be a lonely and stressful time, but there are ways to handle it without turning to medications that can lead you down the road of addiction. Find activities you enjoy doing outside of school. Exercise and eat healthy—you'd be surprised just how much of a natural "high" regular exercise can give you. If you're old enough to get a job or volunteer, do that. Doing things that you find rewarding and enjoyable can go a long way toward helping you manage your anxiety—without using a potentially addictive substance.

Exercise can provide a natural high.

Glossary

Alzheimer's disease The most common cause of dementia in older adults.

anticonvulsant A medication designed to treat seizures.

antihypertensive A medication designed to treat high blood pressure.

antipsychotic A medication designed to treat psychosis, such as in bipolar disorder or schizophrenia.

antisocial Not sociable; antagonistic.

apathy Lack of enthusiasm or interest.

atypical neuroleptics Medication used to treat psychosis, which is a severe mental disorder in which person loses touch with reality.

barbiturate Central nervous system depressant drugs that can produce sedation or anesthesia effects.

cognition A collective term for the mental abilities concerning thinking and knowledge.

compound A mixture made up of two or more elements.

detoxification A process of physically removing toxic substances from the body.

disinhibition A lack of restraint or inhibition.

epilepsy A neurological disorder that causes a person to have seizures.

half-life The amount of time it takes a quantity of a substance to decrease by half.

inhibitors Substances that slow down or prevent a chemical reaction.

muscle tone The normal, resting state of muscle tension in the body.

neurotransmitters Brain chemicals that transmit signals across synapses and throughout the brain and body.

palpitation An abnormally rapid or irregular beating of the heart.

phobia An extremely strong dislike or fear of someone or something.

post-traumatic stress disorder An anxiety disorder that occurs after extreme emotional trauma. The disorder frequently occurs in war veterans.

promiscuous Sexually indiscriminate; having many casual sex partners.

psychopharmacology The study of the use of drugs in treating mental disorders pertaining to mood, sensation, thinking, and behavior.

sedative A drug that reduces irritability and/or excitement, producing a calming effect.

synapse The point where an impulse passes from one neuron to another.

visual-spatial A type of learning or processing characterized by thinking in pictures rather than in words.

Find Out More

Books

Child, Grace. *Prescription Pill Drug Abuse: Dealing with an Adult Child or Teen Pill Addict.* Seattle, WA: Amazon Digital Services, 2014.

Herzanek, Joe. *Why Don't They Just Quit? What Families and Friends Need to Know About Addiction and Recovery.* Seattle, WA: CreateSpace Independent Publishing Platform, 2012.

Lessa, Nicholas, and Sara Gilbert. *Teen's Guides: Living with Alcoholism and Drug Addiction.* New York: Checkmark Books, 2009.

Marshall, Shelly. *Young, Sober, and Free: Experience, Strength, and Hope for Young Adults.* Center City, MN: Hazelden, 2003.

Santasiero, Ronald, and Cherie Santasiero. *Addicted Kids, Our Lost Generation: An Integrative Approach to Understanding and Treating Addiction in Teens.* Seattle, WA: CreateSpace Independent Publishing Platform, 2014.

Above the Influence

www.abovetheinfluence.com

This website provides information and resources to help young people resist drugs.

Just Think Twice

www.justthinktwice.com

The Drug Enforcement Agency created this website to provide a wealth of information about drugs that may be abused by teens and links for people seeking help with an addiction.

Nar-Anon and Narateen

www.nar-anon.org

Nar-Anon and Narateen provide support for drug addicts and people close to them. Narateen is especially aimed at pre-teens and teenagers.

NIDA for Teens

teens.drugabuse.gov/peerx

The National Institute on Drug Abuse created this site to provide information specifically about prescription drug abuse in teens.

About the Author

Cathleen D. Small is an editor and the author of numerous books for Cavendish Square. She is also the mother of two active young boys and two rambunctious pugs. She resides in the San Francisco Bay Area. In her spare time, she enjoys traveling and outdoor activities.

Eating the Alkaline Way

Recipes for a Well-Balanced Honestly Healthy Lifestyle

Natasha Corrett
Vicki Edgson

Photography by
Lisa Linder

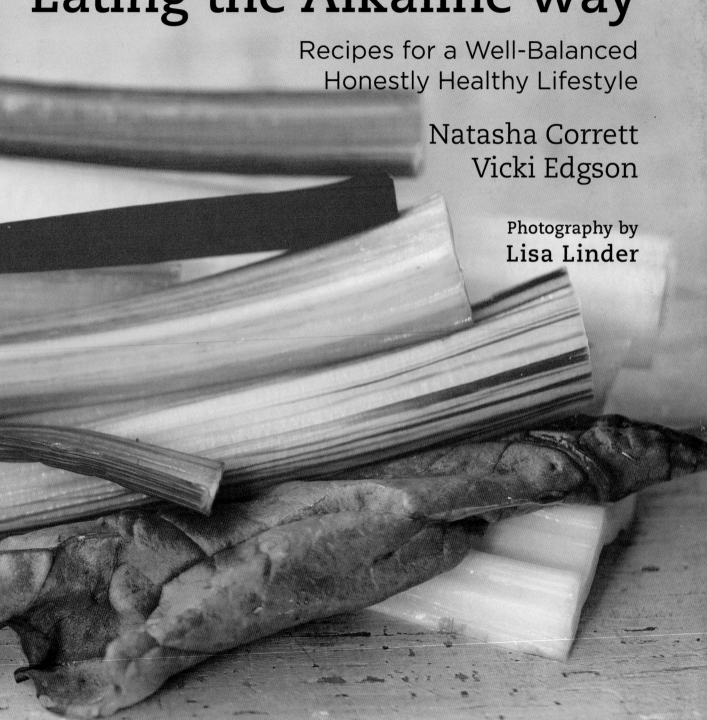

STERLING
New York

An Imprint of Sterling Publishing
387 Park Avenue South
New York, NY 10016

Text copyright © 2013 Natasha Corrett and Vicki Edgson
Design and layout copyright © 2013 Jacqui Small

First published in 2012 as *Honestly Healthy* by
Jacqui Small LLP
An imprint of Aurum Press
7 Greenland Street
London NW1 0ND

ISBN: 978-1-4549-0887-6

Distributed in Canada by Sterling Publishing
c/o Canadian Manda Group, 165 Dufferin Street
Toronto, Ontario, Canada M6K 3H6

For information about custom editions, special sales, and premium and corporate purchases, please contact
Sterling Special Sales at 800-805-5489 or specialsales@sterlingpublishing.com.

Manufactured in China

2 4 6 8 10 9 7 5 3

www.sterlingpublishing.com

From Tash—I dedicate this book to my best friend Laura
who continues to inspire me everyday and to my Mummy
and Daddy who have supported me every step of the way.

From Vix—I dedicate this book to
my dear friend Karen, who first made me realize how
important it is for vegetarians to better understand
how to balance their nutrition for
vital health.

contents

Key to symbols (see page 11)

♥♥♥ really really alkaline food or recipe

♥♥ really alkaline food or recipe

♥ alkaline food or recipe

vegan

Our Story and Passion

We first met on the day of Natasha's birth, when I was introduced to her as her godmother. We have, needless to say, known each other ever since. Our friendship has grown with the years, with Tash always interested to see how my career in nutrition and well-being has grown, while at the same time pursuing her own knowledge of spiritual, holistic, and herbal practises alongside her passion for food—her taste buds having been influenced from an early age by her French restaurateur father.

We both share a passion for great food always starting with raw ingredients. My own mother prepared everything from scratch and I remember the best part of coming home from boarding school was always the smells wafting through from the kitchen. I now experience the same feeling every time I walk into Tash's home—there's always some delicious gluten-free cake on the table, or an extraordinary version of risotto or bean casserole.

We came together in business in May 2009, when I attended one of Tash's retreats in the deep countryside, where she had rented a large mansion for a three-day retreat. At the last minute the chef she had hired let her down and, true to form, Tash rose to the occasion and simply said, "Then I shall have to be the chef!" She proceeded to produce some of the most fabulous vegetarian food I had ever tasted, and the weekend was a resounding success, especially at mealtimes, with everyone exclaiming just how mouthwatering the dishes were. She continued to amaze all of us as meal after meal was produced from seemingly simple ingredients—fresh, tangy, and very tasty.

By the middle of the following week, over half her retreat guests had requested that Tash set up a home-delivery service, and her "Fridge Fill" was launched—three days' worth of breakfast, lunch, dinner, and snacks delivered on a Monday evening. The premise was simply that eating healthy food for at least half your week will yield improvements to your overall health and, in a matter of weeks, have you choosing more carefully when dining out, traveling, or just snacking from your corner store. Tash was adamant that she could start to change the eating habits of the nation by delivering really real food to a handful of people who would spread the word, organically.

"Organic where it matters" became the common thread, and before long the word had indeed spread, and Harrods invited Tash to take a selection of her produce into their store for tasting. She spent a frenetic weekend preparing dishes and painting a wooden crate with her own logo and filling it with straw, as if it had come fresh from the field and ready to serve—it looked divine, tempting, and delicious!

Her presentation to Harrods was a resounding success, and she called me excitedly to tell me the news. I responded immediately with "Do you want an investor in your business? You are clearly going places, and I would love to get involved!"

There followed much excitement, many meetings, and a lot of hard work in prepping our kitchens to match up to the stringent examination procedures that any department store or supermarket deems essential, and we realized we were no longer simply preparing food for friends and clients. The commercial food industry health and safety standards are rigorous (as they should be), and there was much to learn about running our own kitchens.

Interestingly, we never did end up selling into Harrods, as Harvey Nichols and Selfridges both got wind of our brand, and made seductive moves to ply us away! We finally launched into London's Selfridges Food Hall in July 2011, with our own small refrigerated concession, and much fanfare from friends and family. News of our "great, delicious vegetarian food" spread, and we were soon sought by many specialist food shops, stores, and markets.

Tash and I both firmly stand by our brand—the importance of really real food is becoming ever more significant in today's increasingly ready-made, genetically modified range of non-foods, with widening girths, increasing rates of diabetes, and ever-mounting medical bills for diseases that could be avoided if only we *all* ate food as nature intended—in its simplest form. We are both proponents of buying locally sourced, fresh, seasonal produce when possible, and reducing waste by teaching people how to use their food wisely and frugally. We eschew anything that risks being genetically modified, preferring instead to choose an alternative ingredient if we can't be assured that the ones we are using are in their natural state.

We also believe that good food should cost less, but without the knowledge of how to prepare your own from basic ingredients you are forced to pay the market rate for dishes that have been prepared in gigantic kitchens, without love and attention. Food that *is* prepared with love and care *does* taste better—it's an energetic transfer that takes place, and ends up on your tongue, being absorbed in your belly, nourishing the very core of your being. Food is primarily for nourishment, not for punishment or reward, and should be eaten consciously, taking time to be aware of what it affords you and your health. All too often in this frantically busy 21st-century world, we eat while on the hop, or sitting in front of our computers, expecting our digestive systems to "just take care of it," and not realizing that our indigestion, bloated tummies, and constipation are a direct result of our unconscious eating. We want to encourage you to take time over your meals, sit around a table with

friends and loved ones, and appreciate the wonderful offering that is the meal on your plate.

So we have written this book together, combining our experience of great cooking with nutritional know-how to inspire you back into your own kitchen, to sample and savor, simmer and sizzle! We want to encourage each and every one of you to try our simple ethos of taking great raw ingredients, in the right combination, cooked to perfection, to nourish your body and soul. Bon appétit!

The Foundation of Balanced Eating

What is a balanced way of eating in today's terms? We are constantly bombarded with one diet after another, all of which seek to either negate or contradict the other. We may have heard the benefits of the high-protein, low-carbohydrate approach—guaranteed weight loss, apparently safely—but we already know that cutting out any of the major food groups will leave us wanting, eventually.

What we need, and what we are illustrating in this Honestly Healthy program, is to have the right balance of *all* three food groups—that is, carbohydrates, proteins, and fats (see Know your food groups, page 12), in their cleanest and most natural forms—to suit us individually and ensure that we have all the essential nutrients required for healing and repair, rebuilding and energy production on a day-to-day, moment-to-moment basis.

Benefits of an alkaline approach

How often do you find yourself with indigestion after a meal? Or, even worse, knowing that you have eaten too much, or too rich or excessively heavy foods? Reaching for a glass of wine is hardly the answer, with alcohol yet another burden on your body's whole digestive system. Yet this is the pattern of the 21st-century Western diet and it is now recognized as a contributing factor to the types of diseases with which we are increasingly faced—diabetes, heart disease, and cancers.

Many of our frequently chosen foods in the Western diet are acid-forming in the body—that is, when digested they form acidic residues in the bloodstream. Such foods include all meat, dairy produce, and processed, commercial foods in any form, including sugars, breads, cookies, and cakes. In small amounts this is not harmful, but eating acid-forming foods regularly places a heavier burden on the kidneys and liver to break them down further. Both organs require an increase of certain minerals to "buffer" such acidity. For example, additional magnesium is required by the kidneys to alkalize waste matter and, if sufficient amounts of this mineral are not available, stores of magnesium may be leached from bone tissue to support kidney function.

Eating predominantly alkaline food is far easier on the whole digestive system since it matches the pH of the blood, which runs between 7.35 and 7.45. The Honestly Healthy program has been designed to provide vegetarian alkaline foods in balanced combinations to guide you through this new way of eating. You will find that, within a few weeks, you will look and feel lighter, your concentration and memory will have sharpened, your energy levels will have soared, and the quality of your sleep will have improved dramatically.

Eating alkaline means consuming fresh foods as close to nature as possible—organic wholefoods, predominantly vegetarian, with small amounts of legumes and whole grains to supplement an abundance of fruit and vegetables. These can be raw, lightly cooked, or sprouted to create a higher level of protein (see Sprouted beans and seeds, page 34).

Which foods are acid and which are alkaline?

You may be surprised to find that some of the foods you are eating on a daily basis are highly acid-forming (see opposite), contributing to a sense of being over-full, bloated, windy, and uncomfortable. Following a primarily alkaline program will do away with many of these symptoms, virtually overnight. *We are not suggesting that you omit all acidic foods, but rather eat less of them, and ensure that, if you do eat them, you do so alongside plenty of alkaline foods to render the overall meal more alkaline in its total (see also pages 15 and 25).*

Very acid-forming	Mildly acid-forming	Alkaline
STARCHY GRAINS AND VEGETABLES —Breakfast cereals (commercially produced), wheat, gluten-flour breads and pasta, bean (kidney, white), chickpea, peanut butter, pea (dried)	**STARCHY GRAINS AND VEGETABLES**—Buckwheat, corn, lentil, quinoa, millet, oat, rice (white and brown), rye, sweet potato	**STARCHY GRAINS AND VEGETABLES**—Barley, millet, lima bean, soybean (fresh or dried), soy lecithin
FATS AND OILS—Cows' dairy produce (including milk, butter, cheese, yogurt, cream, and ice cream), ghee	**FATS AND OILS**—Brazil nut, caraway seed, cashew, cumin seed, fennel seed, feta, flax seed, halloumi, hazelnut, linseed oil, macadamia nut, peanut, pumpkin seed, sesame seed and oil, sunflower seed and oil, walnut	**FRUITS**—Apple, apricot, avocado, berry (all), cherry, coconut, date, fig, grapefruit, grape, lemon, lime, mango, melon (cantaloupe and watermelon), olives, orange, peach, pear, pineapple, plum, papaya, plums, raisin, rhubarb, tomato (raw)
PROTEIN—Beef, lamb, mutton, pork, rabbit, chicken, duck, goose, turkey, fish, shellfish, egg, seeds (cooked), gelatin	*NOTE: In this book we include foods that are considered to be strictly acid-forming, such as flax seeds, brown rice, or quinoa. We have listed these as "alkaline" (see page 11, pages 16–19) because their nutrient content is so rich that, when combined with plenty of alkaline-rich foods in the same dish, their content is still predominantly alkaline.*	**NON-STARCHY VEGETABLES**—Alfalfa sprout, artichoke, asparagus, bean (green), beet (including the leaves), bell pepper, broccoli, carrot, cauliflower, celery, chard (all colors), dandelion, endive, garlic, greens (winter and summer), horseradish, kale, kelp, kohlrabi, leek, lettuce (all types), mushroom, onion, pea (fresh), radish, sea vegetables (including chlorella, kelp, spirulina, wakame), sorrel, spinach, sprouted seed, sprouts, squash, turnip, watercress, wheatgrass
		FATS AND OILS—Almonds, coconut oil, olive oil
DRINKS AND CONDIMENTS—All alcohol, coffee, cola drinks, soda water, sugar, tea, tonic water		**DRINKS AND CONDIMENTS**—Almond milk, coconut water (fresh), goat's milk (raw), herbal teas (excepting fruit teas), lemon water, soy milk, water (distilled); agave syrup, apple cider vinegar, cayenne pepper, chili pepper, cumin (ground), fresh herbs (all), ginger, honey (raw), lemongrass, lime leaves, mustard seeds and paste, sea salt, tamari sauce, turmeric

What is alkaline?

There are two sorts of alkaline foods, those that are alkaline to digest in the first place, and those that have an alkaline "ash" that is, they become alkaline as a result of being combined with the digestive enzymes produced in the mouth, stomach, and small intestine. These are known as alkaline-forming foods, and can often be wrongly observed as "acidic" to taste—the perfect example of this is lemons and limes, which are acid in taste, but actually very alkalizing (see lists of alkalizing foods on pages 16–19).

All foods need to be broken down into a form of liquid that can then be absorbed through the intestinal wall into the bloodstream, and it is the minerals that each food contains that dictate primarily whether it is predominantly acidic or alkaline. Generally speaking, those foods higher in potassium, magnesium, calcium, sodium, zinc, copper, and iron form a basic ash (that is, in the neutral zone of acid/alkaline, the category into which most natural foods fall).

Simply put, all vegetarian foods such as vegetables and some fruits, nuts, seeds, legumes, and whole grains contain a range of predominantly alkaline minerals and are alkalizing, while animal produce, along with fermented and caffeinated foods and all processed and fried foods, are acid-forming.

The pH spectrum

The pH spectrum is used to measure the acidity/alkalinity of all sorts of substances—stomach acid is pH 1 while ammonia is pH 14. When it comes to food and drink, pH values center around pH 3–9. The higher the pH on the scale below, the more alkalizing the food.

TESTING YOUR PH LEVELS

Measuring your acid-to-alkaline ratio can be carried out with litmus testing papers for either urine or saliva, which you can buy from your local pharmacy. Urine is perhaps more accurate, although saliva is quicker and more easily accessible (it can be done over the counter). Ask your pharmacist for either type of testing papers, but note that you cannot test saliva on a urine-test paper—the color of the litmus will not change.

Urine—The pH of your urine varies according to dehydration and levels of acid-forming foods in the body. Alcohol and caffeine, for instance, substantially change the pH of urine as they are dehydrating and, therefore, make the kidneys work harder to buffer the acidity. Collect a mid-stream sample of urine, dip in the litmus paper strip, and wait for the color change. Compare the color with the indicators on the container to read off your pH. A healthy urine pH is 6.5–7.25.

Saliva—The pH of your saliva also varies according to what you've eaten or drunk within the last couple of hours. To create enough saliva for testing, activate your tongue in your mouth for 30 seconds and then swallow. Repeat this twice before placing a litmus paper strip on your tongue ("rinsing" your mouth in this way will ensure a more accurate reading) and then checking the final color against the indicator on the container to discover your pH. A healthy saliva pH is 6.5–7.5.

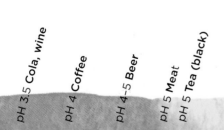

pH 3.5 Cola, wine
pH 4 Coffee
pH 4–5 Beer
pH 5 Meat
pH 5 Tea (black)

pH 6 Milk, commercial breakfast cereal
pH 6.5 Feta cheese, halloumi, buckwheat, dark chocolate
pH 7 Water
pH 7.5 Broccoli, bean, peach
pH 8 Pumpkin, pea (fresh), spinach
pH 8.5 Seaweed, watercress, grape
pH 9 Lemon, watermelon

Alkaline foods

Different foods have different levels of alkalizing power and we find it useful to divide them into three groups, as seen below. In the recipe part of the book, we classify each recipe with an alkalizing rating so that you can pick and choose meals and snacks to help counterbalance acid-forming foods to achieve a more balanced diet and optimum health.

Really Really Alkaline: pH 8.5 to 9

Agar, artichoke, asparagus, avocado, broccoli, cauliflower, cayenne pepper, fennel, grapefruit, grape, kale, kelp and seaweed, kiwi fruit, leek, lemon, lime, melon, pineapple, raisin, spinach, tomato (raw), umeboshi plum, vegetable juice (all), watercress

Really Alkaline: pH 7.5 to 8

Alfalfa sprout, apple cider vinegar, apple, apricot, bamboo shoot, banana (firm), bean (green), beet, bell pepper, cabbage, carrot, celery, daikon radish, date, fig, guava, kohlrabi, lettuce, mango, nectarine, okra, papaya, parsnip, peach, pear, pea (fresh), potato, pumpkin, squash, sweetcorn, tamari, turnip

Alkaline: pH 7 ♥

Almond, amaranth, barley malt, berry (all), Brussels sprout, cherry, chestnut, coconut (fresh water and flesh), cucumber, eggplant, goat's milk (raw), millet, mushroom, olive oil, olive (ripe), onion, pickles, pineapple, radish, sesame seed, soybean, soy milk, sprouted grains, tempeh, tofu, tomato (cooked), vinegar (other than apple cider vinegar, which is the most alkaline of all vinegars)

Know Your Food Groups

There always seems to be confusion over what exactly each food contains, and whether or not it can contain more than one compound—is it a carbohydrate, a protein, or an essential fat, or might it comprise all three? Here we explain the function of each food group, making the whole subject far easier to understand.

What are the types of carbohydrate?

Carbohydrates are the largest of the three groups, with all fruit and nearly all vegetables, as well as grains, falling within this category. They are the energy providers, being broken down into glucose, which is either used immediately for all physical and mental energy or stored in the muscles and liver as glucose and glycogen until needed. Nourishment is required on a daily basis to stay physically and mentally alert, and if you have ever worked out excessively in a gym, or participated in a marathon, you will know how it feels to literally "run out of energy" as your muscles can no longer respond to what your mind is asking them to do. This is why marathon runners "carb-load" in the day or two before the big run. This "running out of energy" rarely happens on a daily basis, unless you are under-nourishing your body, in which case your body will look to your fat stores for energy. *Feeling ravenous is your body's way of telling you that your glucose stores are running on empty—it's time to pay attention and have a meal before you lose concentration or feel physically exhausted.*

However, the different groups of carbohydrates perform a variety of additional functions, and are digested at different rates.

Grains for essential energy production

All grains (barley, buckwheat, millet, oats, quinoa, rice, rye) contain abundant B vitamins, which are vital for energy production at a cellular level. Each cell in your body (particularly muscle cells) contains tiny powerhouses known as mitochondria, which break down the glucose and convert it into energy. The more you exercise, the more mitochondria you develop per cell, increasing the ability to store and utilize energy. This is one of the reasons that fit people feel good—they are literally walking bundles of energy! Time to get off the couch and get moving!

Grains also contain a variety of essential minerals required for muscle movement (think of beating hearts as well as walking and running), breathing, immune function, metabolism, and total body rebuilding and repair. Without grains, the body has to look to its own reserves of fat and lean muscle tissue. Burning fat for fuel is possible, but the energy production in this manner produces a

"dirty" fuel, requiring plenty of antioxidant vitamins to "mop up the mess." This explains why those who lose a lot of fat quickly often don't feel very well—losing fat gradually and consistently is a far healthier and long-lasting approach. On the other end of the scale, super-fit bodies, such as those of marathon runners, need to consume adequate grains in their diet to ensure that their valuable lean muscle tissue is not broken down at a rate faster than it is rebuilt, otherwise they will lose stamina. Muscle tissue contains the highest number of mitochondria of all tissue in the body.

Mental alertness is dependent on the same type of energy production, and it is a misconception that we can "do without" the starch and glucose found in grains. It is estimated that the brain actually uses approximately 70% of the energy released from glucose produced through the breaking down of this specific food group in its normal everyday function (carbohydrates are the main glucose-producing foods). If sitting in a lecture, concentrating on driving, or giving a talk or demonstration, the energy requirements can rise to 85–90% of all the glucose stored, which explains why speakers such as politicians and lecturers often eat immediately after their speech is delivered—they have exhausted their stored energy. You may find that in order to focus on reading this part of the book, you need a quick-fix snack to stay focused—grabbing a banana or a handful of nuts will do the trick.

Many "slimming diets" of late have propounded a low- or no-starch at all approach, meaning that once the fat stores are depleted, the body must turn to breaking down lean muscle tissue for energy. Think of the images you have witnessed of emaciated or anorexic bodies gracing the popular magazines in today's world—these may be thin bodies, but they are not healthy ones! We *need* carbohydrates! This is why many of the recipes in this book contain grains, either in salads, breads, or soups—remember that they are the energy part of the meal.

Simple or complex—that is the question

Whether it be in its wholegrain form (think of oats or millet for oatmeal, brown or red Camargue rice for risotto, or whole quinoa for savory or sweet dishes), or ground into flours for wholegrain pasta, breads, and crackers, these are the complex form of the grain—unaltered and unadulterated. They have the very goodness of the grain left intact, including the fiber, vitamins, and minerals, and have been used for several thousand years as the very staff of life.

Simple carbohydrates, on the other hand, are those that have been bleached, blanched, milled several times to form white flour, white rice, white bread, and all the produce that such processing brings. Commercial cereals, for instance, literally melt on your tongue (as there is no real fiber or goodness left in them!), and mass-produced cookies and cakes require abundant sugars, sweeteners, and other additives to help make them taste like anything. The goodness has literally been wrung out of them, and they have nothing to offer in the way of nutrition. This is why those who start a pack of cookies can rarely stop before the pack is finished, as their body searches for something to convert into energy—contrast this to eating a couple of slices of filling and nourishing pumpernickel bread, and you instantly realize why choosing the complex variety is the only way to go!

Fruits and vegetables for instant energy

Also falling under the carbohydrate banner are fruits and vegetables, providing energy at a more rapidly available rate—think of how quickly you gain momentum after eating a banana or apple at virtually any time of the day. *Fruit that is eaten on an empty stomach is digested in under 20 minutes, with the sugars inherently found in such fruits providing instant glucose for energy.*

Root vegetables, those that grow under the ground (think carrots, white and sweet potatoes, turnips, parsnips, etc), all contain abundant glucose stores, as they derive their goodness and nutrients directly from the moisture in the soil surrounding them. Vegetables that grow sitting on the earth (think butternut squash, pumpkin, and zucchini), gain nutrients from the ground, as well, while deriving energy directly from the sun. They are packed with antioxidant vitamins and minerals, and should form a large part of our daily eating. We include all of these energy-packed ground vegetables in the Honestly Healthy recipes, as we know that the natural sweetness they provide, together with their vitalizing minerals, will satisfy everyone's palate—whether spiced or natural, these foods are essential to the program.

Green vegetables, which grow above ground, have the added benefits of chlorophyll, the deep green color derived from the energy from sunlight that is the "blood" of the plant. Chlorophyll is one of the most alkalizing compounds provided in our food, and should be included, in some form, at least twice a day, in as natural a state as possible.

We believe that these life-enhancing foods should form the major part of your daily meals—alkaline in their natural state, and packed with energy (see also Stacking foods, page 22).

The variety of color and texture in above- or below-ground-growing vegetables is key to providing your body with the widest range of cell-protecting antioxidants, energy-producing glucose, and immune-enhancing minerals.

What are the types of protein?

While all natural food is life-giving, it is the proteins that are *life-building*. All proteins are broken down into amino acids, known as the *building blocks* of life. All animal produce contains the eight essential amino acids we require to rebuild and repair. However, they can be acid-forming in the body, taking days to digest and often putrefying on the way through the digestive system, forming waste products that can be toxic and exhausting, as well as causing bloating and indigestion.

Conversely, vegetarian proteins are found in any food that can be planted to grow into a grain, plant, or tree—in other words, often many, many times the size of the original seed. Think of the transformation of the sunflower seed into the 8–10 ft tall flower—gigantic, given the original size of the seed. These foods are far simpler to digest, and yet yield the same building blocks for every cell in our bodies. It is vital, however, to combine the different sources of vegetarian proteins in order to acquire all eight essential amino acids that together make up our bodies. The perfect analogy for this "building" process is to think of a collection of Lego bricks and the myriad shapes and objects that can be built with their different pieces, colors, and shapes.

THE TRIAD OF PROTEINS

Grains and legumes are important because they provide different types of amino acids, coming together to create total proteins. Legumes include all the beans—butter beans, chickpeas, black-eyed beans, kidney beans—all of which are included in abundance in our recipes, as well as lentils and peas.

All nuts and seeds are perfect protein sources. In your childhood classroom you would have marveled at the fava-bean-in-the-jar session in Elementary Biology—where the two cotyledons (two halves of the bean) split open to allow both the root and the shoot to appear. All beans, nuts, and seeds (as well as most grains) can be sprouted in this way and, as *living food* (literally still growing!), these choices of proteins are the most life-giving, body-building you can have. Including some in your salads on a regular basis will reap numerous benefits—both visible and internal. Nuts and seeds are also vital providers of the essential fatty acids that make up the largest portion of our brains and nervous system (see Fats, opposite).

Soy-based produce is one of the only complete proteins available for the vegetarian, alkaline way. Soybeans (choose non-GM sources) contain all eight amino acids and, in their natural state, preserve them for full use in the body. However, in broken-down form, such as soy sauce, tofu, and tempeh, this complete protein source is actually disrupted, so it is wise to ensure a regular intake of the edamame bean. The only other complete protein from a vegetarian source is blue-green algae, spirulina, and chlorella (see also pages 34–35).

HOW WE RATE OUR GRAINS

Choosing dishes made up from each of the three food groups ensures a broad spectrum of alkaline-forming foods, allowing for excellent variety within the diet. We have rated each recipe in the second half of the book on the basis of its overall alkalinity (see pages 5 and 11 for how we rate alkaline foods and dishes). Using overall alkalinity permits the use of grains such as quinoa, rye, and buckwheat, which are less alkaline, but when combined with highly alkaline foods balance the alkalinity of each dish. Wheat and corn, however, are more acid-forming, which explains why so many people have indigestion, heartburn, burping, and wind, as so much of the Western diet is made up from these grains (think pasta, bread, cakes, commercial cereals, and cookies).

What are the types of fat?

Fats—always a source of anxiety to those who don't understand that some fat is not only good for you, but *essential*—come in various forms.

Fats that are good for you

The simplest way to explain those fats that are good for you is to think of the life-*building* proteins, such as nuts and seeds, and realize that these are usually coupled with (and work in conjunction with) the essential fats found within them. So, sunflower and pumpkin seed oils, macadamia and coconut oils, together with walnut, hazelnut, and olive oils are all beneficial fats, supporting nerve function, mental alertness, concentration, and memory. ***Indeed, some 75% of the brain itself is made up of essential fats.*** Were you to hold a brain in your hands, you would be amazed at how "fatty" an organ it is. Packed with nerves, this brilliant computer in your body is protected and carried within a massive amount of essential fatty acid tissue—miraculous.

In the same way, the insulation of our bodies—the protective layer called our skin—is made up of trillions of cells formed from what is known as a phospholipid bilayer. This is a double layer of essential fats around every cell. It is easy to spot someone on a low-fat/no-fat diet, as their skin is wrinkled and dried, and literally starved of essential fatty acids—just think what their inner organs look like if their outer skin is so parched. Our skin not only insulates us from the heat and cold of our environment, but also envelops our bodies in a protective layer. As the skin is the largest organ of elimination in the body, it is vital to keep its outer layer hydrated with essential fats ingested from within to allow the toxins out. Dehydrated skin lacks not only water but also essential fats to keep each cell supple.

Fats that are bad for you

Saturated fats are found in animal fats—think bacon, sausages, lamb fat, goose fat, cheeses, and so forth. These fats become damaged in the presence of heat, light, and air, and especially in cooking. Research has illustrated that cooked red meat eaten on a regular basis has a role to play in colon cancer—perhaps because it sits partially undigested in the gut for days, but also because of these damaging fats. These fats clog up the arteries, causing heart disease and stroke.

Reversing the damage

Interestingly, the benefits of the essential fats found in nuts and seeds and their oils can *undo* the damage the bad fats have caused. This is because the essential fatty acids, known as omega-3, -6, -9, and -12, are predominantly anti-inflammatory, whereas saturated fats have been found to be pro-inflammatory. Many life-threatening diseases are caused in part by inflammation (see also page 22). We make sure to use several forms of these beneficial essential fats every day, and we also infuse bottles of olive, coconut, sunflower, and hemp oils with herbs, spices, and garlic to create complex flavors for salads and vegetables.

A little word about fish

Much is known about the rich sources of omega-3 essential fats in oily fish, such as tuna, herring, mackerel, and salmon. However, to maximize the fish's full nutritional value, we suggest you buy wild varieties wherever possible and avoid intensively farmed fish.

Alkalinity rating	Nutrients	Benefits to the body
Vegetables		
♥♥♥ Artichoke	Calcium, magnesium, potassium, sodium, folic acid, beta-carotene, vitamins C and K	Diuretic, digestive, contains inulin (stimulates good bacteria in the gut), supports liver, promotes bile flow
♥♥♥ Asparagus	Potassium, folic acid, vitamins C and K, beta-carotene	Kidney-stimulating, mildly laxative, antibacterial
♥♥♥ Broccoli	Calcium, magnesium, phosphorus, vitamins B3, B5, and C, folic acid	Antioxidant, intestinal cleanser, antiviral, antibiotic, stimulates liver function
♥♥♥ Cauliflower	Calcium, magnesium, folic acid, potassium, boron, beta-carotene, vitamin C	Excellent antioxidant, supports liver and kidney disorders, relieves high blood pressure and constipation
♥♥♥ Fennel	Calcium, magnesium, sodium, potassium, vitamin C, folic acid, phytoestrogens	Antispasmodic, relieves cramps, helps to digest fats, good for weight control
♥♥♥ Kale	Calcium, magnesium, phosphorus, potassium, vitamins C, E, and K, folic acid, iodine	Supports thyroid and metabolism, detoxes stomach, improves digestion, stimulates immune system, kills errant bacteria and viruses, potent antioxidant
♥♥♥ Kelp	Iodine, calcium, iron, potassium	Highest source of these minerals, benefits cardiovascular and nervous systems, cleanses toxins, aids digestion
♥♥♥ Leek	Calcium, potassium, folic acid, vitamins A and K	Cleansing, diuretic, eliminates uric acid in gout
♥♥♥ Spinach	Iron, calcium, magnesium, folic acid, vitamins B6 and C	Helps regulate blood pressure, anti-cancer properties, boosts immunity, supports bone health
♥♥♥ Tomato, raw	Calcium, magnesium, phosphorus, folic acid, beta-carotene, vitamin C	Antiseptic, antibacterial, supports liver function, reduces inflammation
♥♥♥ Watercress	Calcium, magnesium, phosphorus, vitamin C, beta-carotene, iron, iodine	Diuretic, breaks up kidney or bladder stones, purifies blood, reduces mucus in digestive and nasal tracts, helps increase metabolism

Alkalinity rating	Nutrients	Benefits to the body
♥♥ Beet	Calcium, magnesium potassium, vitamin C, manganese	Cleansing, reduces kidney stones, detoxes liver and gall bladder
♥♥ Carrot	Calcium, magnesium, potassium, beta-carotene	Cleanses liver, encourages detoxing, supports eye function
♥♥ Celery	Calcium, magnesium, sodium, folic acid, vitamin B3	Helps lower blood pressure, aids digestion, prevents fermentation in the gut, helps prevent arthritis
♥♥ Garlic	Calcium, phosphorus, vitamin C, potassium	Potent antispasmodic, antibacterial, lowers cholesterol
♥♥ Ginger	Calcium, magnesium, potassium, phosphorus	Antispasmodic, anti-nausea, stimulates liver and gall bladder, improves circulation
♥ Onion	Calcium, magnesium, potassium, folic acid, phosphorus, quercetin	Anti-inflammatory, antiseptic, antibiotic, reduces spasms in asthmatics, removes heavy metals and parasites, potent cleanser to digestive tract
♥ Tomato, cooked	Calcium, magnesium, phosphorus, folic acid, beta-carotene, vitamin C	Antiseptic, antibacterial, supports liver function, reduces inflammation

Fruits

Alkalinity rating	Nutrients	Benefits to the body
♥♥♥ Avocado	Potassium, folic acid, vitamins B3, B5, E, and K	High-protein fruit, calming, good for digestion, prevents anemia
♥♥♥ Grapefruit	Calcium, magnesium, vitamin C, potassium	Relieves arthritic pain through salicylic acid, blood cleansing, supports heart health, prevents calcium deposits
♥♥♥ Lemon/lime	Potassium, vitamin C	Dissolves gallstones, potent antiseptic, natural antibiotic
♥♥ Apple	Potassium, vitamin C, beta-carotene, pectin	A tonic, cleansing, lowers cholesterol, removes toxins
♥♥ Date	Calcium, iron, vitamin B3, beta-carotene	Relieves diarrhea, supports respiratory system

Alkalinity rating	Nutrients	Benefits to the body
♥♥ Fig	Calcium, potassium, vitamin C, beta-carotene	Mild laxative, clears toxins, high source of calcium
♥♥ Mango	Vitamin C, beta-carotene, potassium, calcium, magnesium	Reduces acidity, supports kidneys, relieves poor digestion, good blood cleanser
♥♥ Papaya	Calcium, magnesium, potassium, vitamin C, beta-carotene	Potent antioxidant, anti-parasitic, soothes intestinal inflammation, reduces wind, good cleanser
♥♥ Pear	Calcium, magnesium, potassium, folic acid, iodine, pectin	Diuretic, benefits thyroid, stimulates metabolism, pectin removes toxins from gut
♥ Coconut	Magnesium, zinc, potassium, folic acid, vitamin C	Very rehydrating and helps to regulate/support thyroid metabolism in energy production
♥ Pineapple	Calcium, magnesium, potassium, beta-carotene, vitamin C	Antispasmodic, contains bromelain (good for digestion), clears bacteria and parasites

Grains and Pulses

♥ Barley (see page 25)	Potassium, zinc, magnesium, calcium, B vitamins, folic acid	Soothes digestion and supports liver function, heals stomach ulcers, lowers cholesterol
♥ Brown rice (see page 25)	Calcium, magnesium, iron, potassium, zinc, vitamins B3, B5, and B6, folic acid	Calming, mood-enhancing, energizing
♥ Buckwheat (see page 25)	Calcium, magnesium, zinc, potassium, beta-carotene, vitamin C, essential fatty acids, rutin	Grain with complete protein content, supports cardiovascular system and micro-circulation
♥ Chickpea (see page 25)	Calcium, magnesium, potassium, zinc, beta-carotene, folic acid, phosphorus, manganese	Supports kidneys, digestive cleanser
♥ Lentil (see page 25)	Calcium, magnesium, potassium, zinc, folic acid	Good source of alkaline minerals for every organ of the body, neutralizes lactic acid produced in muscles during exercise

Alkalinity rating	Nutrients	Benefits to the body
♥ Quinoa (see page 25)	Calcium, magnesium, potassium, vitamin B3	Gluten-free, high-protein and high-calcium grain with antiviral properties
♥ Soybean	Calcium, potassium, magnesium, vitamins A, C, K, and B3	Complete vegetarian protein, lowers cholesterol, balances hormones

Nuts and Seeds

♥ Almond	Calcium, magnesium, potassium, zinc, folic acid, vitamins B and E	Good protein source, calming, sedating, skin food
♥ Macadamia nut (see page 25)	Calcium, potassium, low sodium, high fiber and high in essential fats (monounsaturated)	Removes toxins, lowers cholesterol, contains anti-aging oils
♥ Sunflower seed (see page 25)	Calcium, magnesium, vitamins A, B-complex, D, E, and K, zinc, manganese, omega-3 and -6 essential fats	Removes toxins and heavy metals from the gut, supports eye health, perfect little buds of protein—more so than eggs, meat, or dairy
♥ Walnut (see page 25)	Potassium, calcium, magnesium, zinc, folic acid, vitamins C and E, omega-3 and -6 essential fats	Supports kidney and lung function, potent source of essential fats for brain, cognitive function, and mood regulation, improves metabolism

Miscellaneous

♥♥ Coconut water	Magnesium, zinc, potassium, folic acid, vitamin C	Very rehydrating, helps to regulate/support thyroid metabolism in energy production
♥ Tofu	Calcium, magnesium, potassium, iron, vitamins A and K	Perfect source of protein for vegetarians, lowers cholesterol, balances hormones

Learn New Eating Habits

When it comes to taking a new approach to healthy eating, it's not just what you eat that matters, it's also the way in which you eat. Do you find you're always grabbing food on the run? Or don't eat for ages and then end up eating too much? So, now is the time for making positive change in both how much and the way you eat so that they become the norm for you.

Choosing the right portion size

There are many ideas around portion sizes, the most prevalent being to measure your portions on scales, or by their fat or calorie content. We don't believe that is either healthy or balanced, and can't imagine how thousands of people are bound by these archaic methods that now bear no relevance to our everyday living. The old ethos of calories in/calories out is over-simplistic, and binds you to your bathroom scales, your tape measures, and your kitchen weights. The only reason we give such detailed measurements in our recipe section is to guide you when you start—we then actively encourage you to experiment according to your own taste—a pinch of this, a spoon of that.

Hand-cupping—*your* hands for *your* stomach

In nutritional terms, we recommend opting for a more manual way of controlling your portion sizes so that you are no longer "bound" to measurements that are so limiting. In the photo on the right, we have shown you the most straightforward way to measure the amount of food that is right for *you*—cup your hands together, and *your* hands will guide *you* to the correct amount for *your* stomach—for it is now known that **the size of one of your hands roughly equates to the size of your stomach (each of us has a stomach shape and size as individual as a fingerprint)**.

While this might look small, if you were to pile your entire meal into your cupped hands and then spread

it on a plate, you would then see that it is more than enough—it is simply that we are used to being served so much more than this in the typical Western diet.

Remember, we are not dieting here—we are creating principles that we can adhere to for life, and trust that it works for each of us, without going into the endless mind conversations—"I shouldn't have that..." or "that was too much..."—that plague too many, mindlessly. To set standard measurements is irrelevant when each of us is so individual—how can a 6'4" man be expected to eat as little as a 5'2" petite woman? Hence *your* hands for *your* stomach.

It is something of a myth that eating excessively stretches the stomach, or that starving does the opposite—if you haven't eaten for a couple of days,

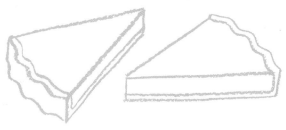

and then do so, your stomach is bound to groan a little. Rather, when you are used to overeating, you probably don't know when you are full as you are likely to be eating "mindlessly" (see Eating conciously, below).

Smaller bowls and plates

We recommend that you build a collection of smaller bowls and plates than you usually use. The fashion has been to serve meals on the largest plates possible, as this resembles restaurant eating, but what one forgets is that restaurants usually serve small portions on large plates to make them look more dramatic! Be honest with yourself and clear out and reorganize your cabinets. Use the extra-large dinner plates as serving plates, and finger bowls as soup bowls. If you are having a one-pot meal (such as Butternut Squash Risotto, page 129), then choose a regular size soup bowl (7-in bowl area with extra for rim) or a small, deep serving bowl (5–6-in diameter) as this is the only dish you will be eating from. A 10-in dinner plate is ample for all the recipes and combination of dishes that we have suggested in our recipe section—and these need not be filled to the edge (see Stacking foods, page 22).

Eating consciously

How often are you aware of what you are eating? Do you stop to savor the look, texture, and color of your food, or do you shovel your meal in as quickly as possible? All too often, we eat on the run, in a furious attempt to "grab and go." Yet this is the worst way we can put food and nourishment into our bodies, as we are doing so in a mindless way—it is no wonder, then, that we aren't aware when we are full. Many people eat far too quickly and don't know when they have had enough. Our bodies are designed with a wonderful mechanism called the vagus nerve, which connects the stomach to the hippocampus, the part of the brain that deals with satiety. **When we eat rapidly, and without concentration, the messages the brain sends via this nerve to the stomach to let us know that we have had enough go largely unnoticed.** Little wonder that we have a society full of seriously overweight people, as we eat sitting in front of the television and our computers. We are simply not *aware*.

The ABC of conscious eating

A—Allocate time to eat, unfettered, and predominantly as an activity in its own right. Aim to set aside at least 20 minutes for a main meal, and preferably considerably more, without engaging in anything other than conversation with others at the table—banish books, newspapers, television, radio, and iPods, and contemplate exactly *what is on your plate*.

B—Be engaged—notice the color, texture, and type of foods in front of you. A meal isn't simply meat, vegetables, and potatoes any more (in this case, there is no meat at all, but plenty of building proteins derived from vegetarian sources, such as nuts, grains, sprouted seeds, soy products, and some cheeses).

C—Chew your foods thoroughly, putting down your knife and fork between each mouthful, rather than shoveling in the next before you have even finished the first. Take sufficient time to ensure that the enzymes in your mouth (secreted by the parotid glands in the base of the mouth, and mixed with saliva) can mix with your food to break it down into almost a liquid. Try this the next time you eat, and ask yourself, "Do I munch, munch, swallow... or do I chew to a juice?" Many yogic practices dictate chewing each mouthful 30–50 times prior to swallowing, to ensure proper digestion. While this is perhaps not practical on a day-to-day basis, the fundamentals of the teaching are sound. No one chokes on liquids, but many do on chunks of food when eating in haste! *This ancient practice of eating mindfully and slowly actually renders a completely different taste to your foods, as chewing and mixing food with enzymes in the saliva renders the food far sweeter than its original components.* This is particularly good for those who feel they are lacking sugary or sweet foods when they start the Honestly Healthy program.

Stacking foods

The important thing in this method is to know how your portions should be split up into the correct balance of carbohydrates, proteins, and essential fats, all of which should be included in each main meal (see right). By including all these food groups in your meal by stacking your foods, you'll eat a healthy and balanced meal each and every time. (See also Know your food groups, page 12.)

Building your stack

With our Stacking method, questions about conscious eating become far simpler—think of it like building a house from the foundation up. See the opposite page for a visual illustration, though note that it's not possible to show the top layer.

Any coconut shavings, nut and seed butters and oils, olive oil or lemon dressings are the coating, providing essential fats for our nervous systems and the suppleness of our inner and outer layers of skin. **10%–15% total of dish**

Nuts, seeds, sprouts, tofu, tempeh, beans, and legumes are the sprinkled third layer of the dish, which provide the very building and repair blocks of our food. These generally take longer to chew, longer to digest and slow down the release of energy from the dish as a whole. **20%–25% total of dish**

Roasted, broiled, baked, steamed, or raw vegetables form the next layer of the stack, providing fiber, vitamins, and minerals that mainly alkalize the whole dish, creating color and contrast (vital not only for the appearance, but also the texture and variety of nutrients contained in the dish). **30%–35% total of dish**

Grains or potatoes always form the bottom of the stack, for example, quinoa, millet, oats, rye, rice, or buckwheat. These complex carbohydrates produce long-lasting energy, providing the very foundation of the stack and the bulk of the dish. **30%–35% total of dish**

Prevention Before Cure

All too often, people wait until illness occurs before changing their eating and lifestyle habits, but we know how *well* you can feel if you take care of yourself and make sure that illness rarely happens. This is a choice and, while it takes time and dedication, the rewards of ongoing good health are so abundant that we want to encourage you to start aiming for great health, rather than simply good health.

How a "dis-ease" is created in the body

Our immunity is vital to our overall health, with an army of different types of immune cells present in our bloodstream, but especially in the digestive tract, as this is our interface with the outside world. *It is estimated that as much as 70% of our total immune cells are present in the gut*—which we experience in a major way when we have an upset tummy or, worse, food poisoning. These immune cells are present throughout the length of our digestive tract from our mouth to our bowels, ensuring that any pathogenic invaders are quelled at the appropriate point or expedited through the system as fast as possible.

Recognizing your body's toxicity

Take a good look at the toxic symptoms in the box to the right and discover how burdened your body's system actually is.

Toxic symptoms
You may be surprised to recognize just how many of these symptoms apply to you:

Headaches/migraines
Joint and/or muscle pain
Indigestion
Heartburn
Bloating
Constipation
Diarrhea
Stomach cramps
Bad breath
Metallic taste in mouth
Sensitive gums
Food intolerances
Excessively painful menstruation
Watery or itchy eyes
Shortness of breath
Sweating
Skin irritations (eczema, psoriasis)
Dry skin
Unexplained hair loss
Lank or dull hair
Acne or constantly spotty skin
Cellulite
Insomnia
Broken sleep
Fatigue
Mood swings
Depression
Lack of motivation
Inability to focus on anything
Irritability
Anger
Sugar cravings
Salty food cravings
Food bingeing

Some of these symptoms can be due to other causes, but by following the Honestly Healthy program for just three weeks, you will find that many of these symptoms simply disappear. Why not invest the time to see for yourself?

Allergies and intolerances may be the key

Food allergies are those reactions that are immediate, severe, and potentially life-threatening, such as swelling of the mouth and lips and closing of the back of the throat, preventing air getting to the lungs. This is called anaphylaxis, and fortunately occurs relatively rarely. However, food intolerances occur far more frequently, sometimes being more difficult to detect as the reaction can occur up to 70 hours or so after the offending food has been eaten. There are several different ways of testing food sensitivities and, generally speaking, blood tests provide by far the most reliable results, as it is in the bloodstream that most reactions occur.

On a more practical level, keeping a detailed "food and symptom" diary may well provide you with some simple answers without having to wait for blood tests to be taken. For example, *if you are suffering from severe headaches on a regular basis, plot a chart over the course of a few weeks of when they occur and see how frequently the foods that you eat almost daily tie in with those.*

Well-recognized links to headaches include chocolate (commercially produced, including sugars and sweeteners rather than the more natural cacao and agave, yacon, and xylitol alternatives included in our recipes), cheese, red wine, and caffeine, all of which contain compounds that are linked with migraines and severe headaches.

Hives and other skin rashes are often associated with strawberries and other red fruits (which can be overly acidic to the body, despite tasting sweet). Lesser-known links include wheat-based products such as bread, cookies, and cakes with fatigue and mild depression; eggs with joint and muscle aches and pains; and mushrooms, yeast, and molds with chronic fatigue, perpetual flu-like symptoms, and low energy and mood. What is going on here?

The answer is *inflammation*

Inflammation is now considered to be the major cause of most chronic diseases, including heart, cardiovascular, lung, and digestive problems, as well as skin issues. Inflammation of *any* tissue in the body attracts extra fluid to the site, and an imbalance of electrolytes (such as sodium, potassium, calcium, and magnesium) at a cellular level is commonly found as a result of such inflammation. It is precisely this electrolyte balance that the body is seeking to maintain on a moment-to-moment basis.

Top foods for alkaline energy

We list our top foods, which are included in most of our recipes, with their alkalinity ratings and what they do for your body on the tables on pages 16–19. We always aim to create menu plans that are high in variety and balanced in acid/alkaline content, looking for the magic 80:20 rule—aiming to eat approximately 80% alkaline foods with each meal, or during each day, will go a long way toward ensuring that you are supporting your body's natural functions. We don't have to keep repeating it—you just have to try it!

Magic minerals

The minerals calcium, magnesium, potassium, and phosphorus are found in all alkaline foods, and these are the vital minerals for regulating the pH of the body's fluids. Calcium and magnesium also work in balance to regulate the beat of the heart, the building of bone and ligaments, the regulation and response of the nervous system, cognitive function, and mood. Both iron and iodine are required for blood transport, for cardiovascular health, and for metabolism, which is regulated by the thyroid gland.

Perfect proteins

It is important to note that protein is found in any nut, seed, or grain that can be planted and will grow into a tree or flower that is substantially larger than the seed—remember that sunflower, which is many thousands of times larger than the seed it originated from. Soybeans and tofu provide all eight essential amino acids for rebuilding and repair, strong immunity and energy production.

In some recipes in the book, you will see that we have included foods that are considered to be acid-forming, such as brown rice, quinoa, lentils, or macadamia nuts. We have listed these as "alkaline" in the tables on pages 16–19 and include them because their nutrient content is so rich that, when placed with plenty of alkaline-rich foods in the same dish, the combined, or average, alkaline content is still predominantly alkaline. Nature would never have supplied us with these foods had they not had their own benefits. This is a perfect example of when to allow some of the acid-forming foods into your program—we use some non-cows' dairy produce, such as feta and halloumi, as these are less acid-forming than cows' dairy and provide essential calcium and minerals—but always serve these alongside really really alkaline vegetables, dressings, or salads. Remember, the more natural the state of the food, the higher the alkaline content.

How an alkaline state can help to cure ailments

Eating a highly acid-forming, animal-protein-based diet may lead to intestinal inflammation (ulcerative colitis, irritable bowel syndrome (IBS), and Crohn's disease all being at the worst end of the spectrum), as well as chronic rhinitis and skin problems (such as eczema and psoriasis). As meat is difficult to digest, and dairy- and wheat-based foods are commonly eaten daily, it is no wonder that so many people are plagued by a collection of minor illnesses. Sadly, few doctors understand—or even know of—the connection between the foods we choose to eat and the illnesses that occur as a result.

The good news is that once we know how to balance acid and alkaline foods in our diet, massive change can take place. Within a matter of days of removing foods that are causing either inflammation or intolerances, aches and pains start to disappear as the body starts to heal and repair. This is why we recommend the Cleanse phase (see pages 32–37), whereby *all* the potentially offending foods and drinks are removed, toxins are reduced in the environment around you, and an abundance of life-giving, energetic foods (such as hemp seed, chlorella, and spirulina) are recommended to cleanse the body and alkalize the system; and subsequently the Lifestyle phase (see pages 38–42), which is a program for life, to ensure increasingly good health.

Alkalizing foods begin by literally "balancing" each cell in the body, supporting its natural energy production and waste-clearing processes by creating the correct electrolyte balance of sodium and potassium. Without getting too technical, the vitality of a cell depends upon sufficient nutrients to allow it to function at its best, and this happens far more readily in an alkaline environment. If the fluids surrounding each cell are too acidic, the sodium/potassium balance is thrown into disarray, causing cellular dehydration. When we talk about "hydrating" the body, we don't just mean "drink plenty of water"—we are talking about nutrient-rich juices, green smoothies, and alkalizing pH drops to add to your water. These are now readily available in most health food stores and online worldwide (see Directory of food suppliers, page 192).

Take the test and see!

We recommend that you drink at least two juices daily over a period of ten days to evaluate improvements to whatever is troubling you at present—headaches, recurrent colds and infections, aches and pains. As your body starts to rebalance its pH levels, your symptoms will start to diminish and the power of eating the alkaline way will be revealed.

What's Your Fix?

It is inevitable that there are some foods you will find hard to give up—it is little wonder, as they were designed to be addictive in the first place! If you think of the cocktail of sugars and sweeteners, additives and salt included in commercial cereals or breads, for example, the flour and the water used to bring them together are almost incidental when you read the ingredients list!

However, it *is* important to look carefully at just how much of these types of foods you consume on a daily basis, and this is especially relevant when looking at the acid/alkaline balance, for most of these ingredients are acid-forming—and the irony is that it is partly the fact that they *are* acid-forming that makes them so addictive. **By embarking on a predominantly alkaline eating program, you will find yourself less drawn to them in the first place, and they will eventually become totally unappealing as your palate changes.**

Food addictions and cravings are usually indicative of a body out of balance and signify specific nutrient deficiencies. While most vitamins are readily available in all fruits and vegetables, it is the minerals in whole grains, nuts, and seeds, as well as soy products, that nourish us at a cellular level, leaving us feeling satisfied, calm, and yet energized. Getting off the junk-food gravy train is key to feeling fantastic, and it deserves the time and effort it initially takes to wean yourself off such foods in order to gain the benefits.

Acknowledging your triggers

Most of us have specific situations that trigger eating "quick-fix" foods with no real value to us, and it is important to identify them so you can be prepared for the eventuality and provide better choices.

Ask yourself which negative emotions (such as being bored, tired, or premenstrual) or particular situations (such as working late or skipping breakfast) are most likely to cause you to pick up a packet of cookies, chips, bar of chocolate, or salted nuts, alcohol or carbonated drinks, or yet another coffee. It may be that you experience such emotions

or situations on a regular basis, and frequently give yourself excuses for "needing" or "deserving" a treat. But are these foods and drinks really treats, and do they make you feel better at all?

The important thing to remember is that any foods or drinks that give you an instant boost are likely to leave you feeling lower than before you ate or drank them. This is because any additives, sugars, and sweeteners, caffeinated drinks, and other stimulants interfere with the delicate balance of your blood-sugar regulation. This leaves you on a perpetual roller coaster of highs and lows, always ending on a low—more tired, more irritable, and less motivated to take care of yourself properly.

Start your day as you mean to go on

We recommend that you start your day with a tonic of alkaline goodness. There is nothing more effective than a green smoothie or juice in the morning for regulating blood-sugar levels from the outset (see pages 24 and 46–48). Adding a small amount of protein to your juice, such as ground hemp seed or flax seed, will prolong the release of energy that you derive from such a drink, and prevent the peaks and troughs associated with strong coffee or tea. How you start your day determines how the rest of the day will work for you, as choosing croissants or toast and marmalade will have you reaching for more of the same for the next few hours, eventually leading to fatigue and inability to concentrate. It only takes a few minutes to prepare a fresh juice and ours are designed to be a whole meal in themselves.

Having your cake and eating it too

Looking through our Breads section (see pages 160–163), you will realize that good-quality, wholegrain breads, made without sugar and using sweeteners such as cinnamon, nutmeg, coconut, and agave syrup, allow you to indulge in delicious alternatives, rich in B vitamins for energy and minerals that support the immune, nervous, and cardiovascular systems. Where these recipes also include nuts and seeds, the protein will provide you with longer-lasting energy, and cooking them at a low temperature preserves the essential fatty acids inherent in all nuts and seeds.

Banishing the chocoholic blues

Cacao, the raw ingredient used to make all chocolate, actually contains abundant nutrients with potent antioxidant properties that protect our cells from damage. It is also a rich source of magnesium, which helps us to relax and generally provides a feel-good factor. Cacao is bitter to taste, which is why sugar is added to commercial chocolate bars and candies. This is especially a requirement for milk chocolate, to prevent the rancidity of the dairy solids. It is the sugar, not the cacao, that is so addictive, and obviously provides no benefit.

We love cacao—hence the abundance of recipes that include this beneficial ancient ingredient, first discovered in South America thousands of years ago. (See Treats and Snacks, page 148 and Desserts, page 168.)

Leave salt to the sea and the Himalayas

Salt was first used to preserve meats and fish in an age when refrigerators hadn't been invented, and when fishermen went to sea for several weeks at a time. This is no longer the case, and we are now fastidious about ensuring that use-by dates are not exceeded and we have the luxury of being able to buy fresh food daily. Most vegetables contain appropriate levels of salt and nutrients (see the tables on pages 16–19), and it should not be necessary to add any or much to your cooking. Use herbs and spices instead to provide additional flavor. Himalayan salt, used in the recipes, is mineral rich and balances sodium with many other vital nutrients, helping to create a better balance in your body, and not posing the threat of dehydration. Most commercially produced salt is processed, stripping out many of the other essential minerals, whereas the salt from the Himalayas is centuries, if not millennia, old.

Cravings for salt usually indicate a deficiency in minerals—especially zinc, which helps to regulate the sensitivity of our taste buds, as well as being vital for strong immunity and to support adrenal function, which regulates our response to stress. This latter point explains why you might opt for salty snacks when you are overtired and stressed—when you would actually be better off having brown rice, quinoa, or barley couscous with pumpkin and sunflower seeds to boost zinc stores.

Good fizz, bad fizz

Real champagne from Champagne in France has had nothing added to it to make it fizz—the fermentation method and the way the bottles are turned create the bubbles. The bubbles you find in cans of cola are purely synthetic, created by a cocktail of chemicals and aeration. How this behaves in the body is to affect the nervous system, pepping you up artificially, with the inevitable subsequent drop in energy as your blood-sugar levels are again disrupted. *The only natural ingredient in a can of cola is water!* Why not have naturally carbonated water with a few slices of ginger, a stick of lemongrass, or a sprig of fresh mint leaves to pep you up? Adding a pinch of cayenne pepper to water will give you more energy than you need, and supergreen powders including spirulina and chlorella provide the highly bioavailable nutrients your body needs, as well as being very, very alkaline.

Caffeine—good or bad?

While coffee is a natural bean, the caffeine it contains does more harm than good in the long term. *The occasional freshly ground coffee is not disruptive, but daily consumption leaches essential minerals from bones and other tissues in the body to buffer the kidneys in its elimination.* The caffeine added to colas is synthetic and far more damaging, interfering with the nervous system and seratonin/dopamine pathways—it is virtually a depressant when excessively consumed.

Breaking habits

A habit is something you have ground into place simply through repetition, and deciding to break it is nothing more than a choice. The fears of "how will I feel" or "how will I manage without" can only be diminished by actually making the decision to stop what is harmful to you by replacing the habit with a better choice. There's no time like the present.

Some foods and drinks are so toxic that ceasing to consume them can cause headaches and some muscle aches and pains, but these last only for a few days and exercising speeds up the process of ridding the body of those damaging chemicals. This is what the Cleanse does—clears your body of toxic residues that end up stored in fat cells and which hinder your performance.

It's All About Upgrading

Upgrading is a term we came up with for motivating our friends and clients to make small but significant changes to their eating habits, one step at a time, rather than thinking of the mountain-like challenge of throwing everything out in one go and having to start sprouting their own seeds on day one.

We like to think of it as the same experience as choosing to upgrade your plane ticket from economy to business—while it might cost you a little more in time and effort, the comfort, health improvements, and nourishment you will get from this kind of attention will yield its benefits ten-fold. Good food doesn't necessarily cost more. By buying fresh ingredients in local markets you are supporting local and specialist farmers rather than endless imports from overseas; you are buying in season; you are thinking more carefully about the balance of your foods, and what goes with what—in other words, you are probably buying less and making more out of it.

What to upgrade first?

Upgrading can be done in phases or stages, so that you feel in control of exactly what changes you are making, and are able to perceive the benefits as you go. *Prioritizing your specific health complaints, and focusing on those in the first instance will yield huge rewards.* For example, if you frequently suffer from colds and chest infections, chronic rhinitis, or other ear, nose, and throat problems, it would be best to start with changing your dairy milk intake to nut milks (almond, Brazil nut, and macadamia, for example—see pages 53 and 57), soy or feta and halloumi cheeses and soy yogurts, as it is often the whey content of cows' dairy that irritates the mucus lining of the nose, throat, and chest endothelial linings. You will observe positive changes literally within days, and your energy levels will build as the stress of the intolerance to the dairy foods dissipates.

On the other hand, if you are suffering from irritable bowel syndrome (IBS), bloating, and frequent pain or wind in the abdominal cavity, you would be best to cut out all wheat and yeast-based breads, pastas and noodles, as well as cookies, cakes, etc. This book is literally full of wheat- and gluten-free foods throughout each recipe section, from breakfast pancakes and granola to chocolate brownies and coconut bread, to buckwheat or rice noodles. For most people, even those who don't suffer from IBS or related discomfort, the health benefits of cutting out commercial breads and cookies, daily sandwiches and pasta will be immeasurable—and worth the effort for all.

Cook yourself healthier

By making some simple swaps (see opposite) you can make super-nutritious food for yourself in minutes. Don't fret about making everything from scratch initially—search out ready-made varieties of the "improved" option, before going on to make your own.

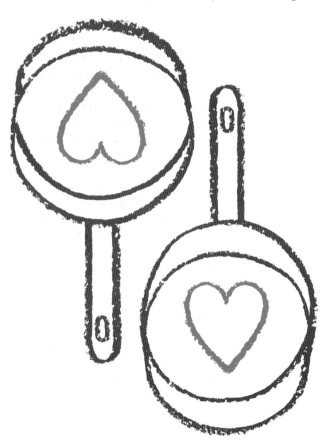

Simple but Smart Upgrades

From Ready-made bottled juices
To Freshly made juices or blended green drinks
Benefits Pulped juices made at home from whole greens, fruits, and vegetables contain all the cholesterol-lowering fiber that is stripped away in commercial juicing, as well as retaining the full vitamin content if consumed within one day.

From Ready-made smoothies
To Homemade versions with soy or nut milks, fresh fruits, and added hemp or flax seed
Benefits The soy or nut milks provide a good level of non-cows' dairy calcium and protein, without the sugars that are often added to the supermarket varieties. Flax and hemp seeds provide extra essential fatty acids that benefit the nervous system, memory, and skin and regulate hormones.

From Ready-made muesli, yogurt, and granola
To Nutty granola and berries (see page 56)
Benefits Soaking the oats for the muesli activates the enzyme content of the grain, raising the protein content and making it more easily digested and absorbed, plus it has a lower glycemic index.

From Ready-made soups
To Homemade soups with added legumes
Benefits Countless! Far higher mineral and vitamin content, variety, and alkalinity—homemade soups allow for using up the stray vegetables from other recipes, as well as the increased protein content from beans and legumes, usually only found in very low content in supermarket-bought versions.

From Ready-made lasagne
To Homemade vegetable bake
Benefits Fresher vegetables and no salt or other additives required to "hold" a commercial version together for appearance. Homemade allows you to create your own topping—crushed nuts, oats, and seeds make delicious and nutritious toppings.

From Ready-made pasta salads
To Homemade quinoa, brown rice, or buckwheat-noodle salads or mixed grain and root vegetable salads with feta or smoked tofu and seeds, nuts, and other toppings
Benefits The minerals in the home-cooked wholegrain quinoa and buckwheat are far higher than commercially produced pasta, and these grains do not cause bloating.

From Ready-made salad dressings
To Selection of fresh, homemade dressings to store in the fridge
Benefits Nothing beats a fresh dressing for flavor and variety. Commercial versions contain additives, sugar, and salt to give them a long shelf life.

From Tea and coffee
To Fresh ginger, lemongrass, fennel, and peppermint teas; dandelion root or chicory coffee granules (available in all good wholefood stores)
Benefits Stimulating fresh ingredients that naturally give you a lift, without the subsequent come-down that caffeine provides. No anxiety and no cellulite (caffeine is stored in fatty tissues and is a known cause of orange-peel thighs and bottoms).

From Sliced white bread or croissants
To Commercial rye or pumpernickel breads, sunflower or pumpkin-seed flatbread, homemade rye soda or coconut breads (see page 60), buckwheat wraps and pancakes
Benefits Omitting commerically produced yeast breads lowers your intake of sugars and salt. Wholegrain breads have a far higher vitamin and mineral content. Tastier, and far more satisfying.

From Ready-made puddings
To Homemade ice creams or cakes
Benefits No sugars or addictive additives. Packed with fresh fruits and nut milks for protein. Unbeatable versus unbearable—no contest!

The Honestly Healthy Cleanse

Many consider cleansing to be something the body does naturally, by itself—which indeed it does. However, with the total toxic load of the commercially produced foods we consume, drinks we imbibe, and airborne chemicals we are exposed to on a daily basis, it is little wonder that we need to address this toxicity in a more strenuous way several times a year.

When to embark on a Cleanse

We recommend carrying out a Cleanse with the change of the seasons—when the temperature changes and your body is adapting to this. The body is designed to adapt to seasonal changes.

To be clear, the Cleanse is *not* what others call a detox. Our bodies are eliminating through urine, feces, and sweat on a moment-to-moment basis, and the liver has its own complex detoxification system. However, the Cleanse *is* a way of supporting your body's natural systems in these processes, by providing nutrient-dense drinks and foods that are all known to have elimination-enhancing properties.

How long should you Cleanse for?

Your Cleanse can last between five days and three weeks, depending on how much you want to change your eating habits. For your first Cleanse, aim for seven to ten days and see how you feel. If you are bounding with energy (which we are pretty sure you will be), then continue for another week, before moving on to the Lifestyle phase of the program (see page 38).

The first stage of the Cleanse is to remove all those foods and drinks you have been consuming in a regular or addictive pattern (see What's your fix?, page 27), to lighten the load on your digestive system. If coffee is your drug of choice, you will be going without; if a pain au chocolat is your morning fix, you will quickly notice how different you feel without it.

Cooking methods for the Cleanse

Steaming, stir-steaming ("frying" food at a lower temperature with water to create steam), gently simmering, and, best of all, raw and/or marinated in lemon juice and olive oil are the preferred cooking methods for all vegetables, as these are most nutritious. During the Cleanse, avoid stir-frying, baking, or roasting vegetables as higher temperatures can lower the overall nutrition of a dish.

Preparing to embark on your Cleanse

Plan your Cleanse by ensuring that you will have plenty of time to relax and will not have to attend business functions and parties, where you are unlikely to be able to find the correct foods and may be tempted into eating the foods you know are not recommended. Ideally, you want to have time for light daily exercise—yoga and pilates, swimming and dance are all perfect as they involve using all the body muscle groups, and in particular stimulate the digestion to help eliminate toxins more efficiently.

Allocating time to ensure you have sufficient foods in your fridge on a daily basis is the key to the success of the Cleanse. Follow the menu planner (see page 36) to start with, so you know what you are having each day. You will not go hungry if you aim to eat every two to three hours—a juice, smoothie, soup, or salad—for the first two days. Thereafter, you can space out your consumption to every three to four hours, as your body is absorbing highly bioavailable nutrients from your meals. Keep your fluid intake high to minimize cravings for the first few days.

The benefits of being more alkaline will start to appear within a matter or days. *You will be able to think more clearly, sleep more soundly, have greater levels of energy and concentration than you have had for some time. Your skin will brighten, your eyes will sparkle, and there will be a new spring in your step.* Internally, your immune system will respond by clearing out old ills—viruses may reappear, but not for long, as the immune army will start to strengthen, and you will feel fitter than you have for a long time.

Repeating the Cleanse up to four times in the first year, as the seasons change, is ideal. After the Cleanse, you can move on to the Lifestyle phase, expanding the variety of foods you can eat and choosing from a vast array of recipes in the second part of this book. Enjoy!

Foods to avoid during the Cleanse

We recommend cutting out the following altogether during your Cleanse:

Red meat, chicken, turkey, duck, all eggs, fish, and shellfish
Reason These foods are predominantly acid-forming and can take 2–4 days to go through your digestive tract—we are aiming for fast-moving foods to cleanse your system.

Most dairy produce (goat's milk and cheese, ewe's halloumi and feta are included in the Lifestyle, but NOT on the Cleanse)
Reason Acid-forming, and most animal-based dairy produce is mucus-forming in the respiratory and digestive tracts, which interferes with nutrient absorption.

Coffee, tea, cola drinks, carbonated water
Reason All acid-forming and a stress to the adrenal glands; also inhibit nutrient absorption. Contain tannins and artificial colorings, which often contribute to headaches and migraines. Carbonated waters are often high in sodium.

Sugar in any form
Reason Acid-forming and produces blood-sugar highs and lows, creating artificial bursts of energy followed by fatigue. Also feeds pathogenic bacteria in the gut, which cause wind, bloating, fatigue, headaches, muscle aches and pains.

All breads, cakes, and cookies containing gluten-flour (wheat, oats, rye, and barley)
Reason While oats, rye, and barley are all highly nutritious grains in their own right, they do contain gluten—the protein portion of the grain—which tends to create a "sticky" mass in an already bunged-up digestive tract. Beneficial grains are important during the Lifestyle, but not during the Cleanse.

Couscous, semolina, spelt (all wheat-based grains)
Reason Highest gluten-containing grain, prevents cleansing through the digestive system.

Lentils, oats, peanut butter, kidney beans, chickpeas
Reason Low-alkaline and slow to digest. These are all beneficial during the Lifestyle but NOT on the Cleanse.

All commercial breakfast cereals
Reason Over-processed, high in sugars, salt, and other additives. Burden on kidneys to break down chemicals.

All rice (brown, red, and basmati)
Reason Slow to move through the digestive tract.

All take-out and convenience foods
Reason Excessive additives and over-processing place additional burden on the digestive tract to "break down" the foreign items contained in such foods.

All packet snacks
Reason Deep-fried and salted, they stimulate the kidneys to work overtime, dehydrating the body and unbalancing the minerals sodium and potassium.

All condiments—for example, ketchup, sauces, vinegars, mustard, and pickles
Reason Acid-forming and unbalancing the minerals sodium and potassium.

Alcohol—including all wines, spirits, and fermented after-dinner drinks and digestifs
Reason All alcohol is sugar-forming in the gut and disruptive to the body's natural blood-sugar regulation. Alcohol stimulates sugar and carbohydrate cravings, as well as interfering with nutrient absorption.

Foods to enjoy during the Cleanse

The majority of foods that you will be consuming are vegetable-based, as these are rich in nutrients that support cleansing at a cellular level, as well as providing the fiber required to clean the digestive tract thoroughly. *These may all be eaten raw or cooked, but the closer to their natural state they are, the more intact and undisturbed the nutrients will be.*

Dark green leafy vegetables

Curly kale, Savoy cabbage, spinach, arugula, watercress, parsley, cilantro, summer and winter greens, and broccoli are excellent in juices (see Cleansing juices, page 37, and Green smoothies, page 46), with salads and simply steamed vegetables as part of a meal.

The allium family of vegetables

Known for their cleansing and liver-supporting properties, onions, leeks, garlic, and scallions all contain the amino acid L-cysteine, upon which the liver is dependent for safely clearing certain foods and toxic substances. Steaming onions, leeks, and garlic sweetens them, and adding them raw to juices and smoothies packs a huge immune-supporting punch.

Supergreens

Much is written about the power of the microscopic blue-green algae found in the untainted Klamath Lakes in Oregon, which some believe hold the only toxin-free waters left on the planet. This algae is possibly the richest source of vegetarian nutrients to be found, and many have fasted for several days drinking these living algae and water alone.

We don't advise that you go to such drastic measures, but we do encourage you to have ½ teaspoon of powdered algae dissolved in 2–4 cups water per day, either combined with other juices or as a stand-alone drink. The higher the concentration of algae to water, the richer the nutrient shot—try it and see for yourself.

Sprouted beans and seeds

By far the most nutrient-dense options during the Cleanse, adding sprouts to your daily regime will provide you with the best protein/vitamin/mineral combinations, and these "living foods" will have you bursting with energy. Remember to dress them only with olive oil or nut/seed oils, such as walnut, hazelnut, or pumpkin seed, together with lemon or lime juice, but no vinegars. Choose organic varieties that are fresh and green (avoid any that have gone brown at the tips). Best of all, buy a stack of sprouting trays and sprout your own—always so satisfying. The best beans to sprout are mung, soy, alfalfa, lentils, and split peas.

Fruits

The only fruits recommended during the Cleanse are apples, lemons, grapefruits, and limes as these are the most alkalizing. Some avocados can be included, as these provide excellent protein, vitamin E, and essential fats, but should not be eaten every day as they are rich.

Apples support the liver and gall bladder in their inherent cleansing roles. Add whole apples to juices to provide a little sweetness, if you like, and also for their pectin, contained just under their skin, which helps to latch onto toxins in the gut and remove them with the additional fiber. All other fruits, including berries, should be reserved for the Lifestyle phase.

Spirulina

Considered to be as potent as blue-green algae (see Supergreens, opposite), spirulina is one of the smallest single-cell plants, packed with iron and B vitamins, including B12 (very important for vegetarians, as this essential B vitamin is often lacking in their diet). Research has found that the immune-boosting and liver-cleansing properties of spirulina are superb and multifaceted, so adding a teaspoon of the dried powdered variety to your juices and cold soups is well worth it! Do not heat spirulina, as the nutrients are easily damaged in such a microscopic entity.

Sea vegetables

Seaweeds, such as wakame, kelp, nori, and kombu, are all alkalizing, and contain calcium, potassium and iron. They are considered essential in the macrobiotic approach to eating —introduced to the West some 50 years ago by Japanese Michio Kushi. The macrobiotic approach takes vegetarianism to an extreme and can be difficult to adhere to in everyday life, as it is hugely time-consuming to prepare. For the Cleanse, you can buy some of these seaweeds fresh, but soaking dried varieties and adding them to juices, smoothies, and soups is beneficial, as they are known to remove toxins rapidly and settle the digestion.

Dairy alternatives

While several nut milks (see pages 53 and 57) are favored in the Lifestyle part of the Honestly Healthy program, only almond milk is recommended during the Cleanse, as it is really alkaline and contains an abundance of magnesium, which is relaxing to body and mind and encourages more rapid movement of foods through the digestive tract. Making your own almond milk takes only a little time and is preferable to commercial varieties, which are often sweetened. When choosing soy milk look for organic varieties. Rice milk is *not* suitable for the Cleanse, although you can use it occasionally in the Lifestyle phase, providing the milk is derived from brown rather than white rice.

Hemp seed, flax seed, and pea protein powders

Nowadays these protein-rich ground seeds and peas are all readily available in most supermarkets. The essential fatty acids found in hemp seed and flax seed are potently anti-inflammatory and add considerable mineral value to juices and soups. They can also be added to soy-based smoothies for rebuilding and repair, as their zinc, calcium, and magnesium content are excellent.

Herbal teas

As most of the Cleanse period involves drinking juices and soups and eating predominantly raw food salads, it is vital to ensure you drink plenty of fluids to help you stay hydrated. Stimulating teas such as ginger and fennel are excellent for supporting the liver's natural cleansing. We recommend that you have a rotation of about four or five teas daily, so you do not over-stimulate any of the cleansing organs unnecessarily. Remember that hot water with lemon or lime is by far the most alkalizing of all hot drinks, and making a pot to provide three or four cups first thing in the morning is ideal to get your digestive system moving beautifully. Do not drink either green or white teas on the Cleanse, but save these slightly caffeinated, yet highly antioxidant varieties for the Lifestyle phase instead.

Menu Planner for the Cleanse Phase

DAY 1

Morning
Lemon and hot water upon rising
The Ultimate Morning Wake-up
smoothie (page 47)
Quinoa Porridge with Macadamia
Nut Milk (page 53)

Lunch
Falafel Wraps with salsa and yogurt
(page 70)

Snack
Spinach and Chickpea Hummus
with Raw Flax Seed Crackers
(page 167)

Dinner
Mixed Vegetable and Soybean
Hotpot (page 82)

DAY 2

Morning
Lemon and hot water upon rising
Toxin Reducer juice (page 37)
Buckwheat Pancakes (page
52) with soy yogurt instead of
blackberry compote

Lunch
Dill Steamed Artichokes (page 75)
with a fresh green salad

Snack
Beet and Walnut Dip (page 166)
with gluten-free crackers

Dinner
Fennel and Pear Soup (page 80)

DAY 3

Morning
Lemon and hot water upon rising
Liver Love juice (page 37)
Raw Buckwheat and Cinnamon
Granola (page 54) with Almond
Milk (page 57)

Lunch
Watercress, Roasted Onion, and
Pistachio Salad (page 88)

Snack
Smoky Eggplant Dip (page 166)
with fresh vegetable crudités

Dinner
Layered Vegetable Bake (page 112)

DAY 4

Morning
Lemon and hot water upon rising
Fresh smoothie (page 46)
Nutty Granola (page 56) with
Almond Milk (page 57)

Lunch
Spicy Tofu Skewers (page 12?)
and Mint-and-Mango Marinated
Zucchini Spaghetti (page 126)

Snack
"Cheesy" Kale Chips (page 159)

Dinner
Portobello Mushroom and Fennel
Salad (page 100)

DAY 5

Morning
Lemon and hot water upon rising
Hydrator juice (page 37)
Avocado on Toast (page 49) with
a poached egg

Lunch
Butternut Squash Soup (page 79)

Snack
Nut butter (page 160) with
raw crudités

Dinner
Tomato and Mushroom Dhal (page
127) with Sweet Tomato Tabbouleh
(page 146)

Cleansing Juices

The importance of hydration cannot be overestimated during the Cleanse phase. The recipes below contain a wide variety of nutrients that support liver, kidneys, and bowel to clear the backlog of toxins you have accumulated. They help to keep energy up and sugar cravings down.

Toxin Reducer

1 fennel
½ cucumber (or 1 small)
1-in piece of fresh ginger
juice of ½ lemon
1 green apple

Liver Love

1 large beet
2 handfuls of spinach
3 carrots
½ handful of flat-leaf parsley

Hydrator

1 handful of broccoli
1 pear
2 celery stalks
1 sprig of mint

Immune Booster

3 beets
2 red apples
1-in piece of fresh ginger
juice of ½ lemon

Green Goddess

2 apples
1 handful of kale
½ cucumber
1 handful of watercress

To make any of these juices, simply blend the ingredients in a juicer until smooth.

The Honestly Healthy Lifestyle

Having completed the Cleanse phase, you will now understand what it's like to think more clearly, have more energy, wake up feeling refreshed, and have the motivation to take on board the principles described earlier (see Know your good groups, page 12, and Learn new eating habits, page 20).

We don't say you have to aspire to eating in perfect balance 100% of the time—instead, we encourage you to look to nourishing yourself most of the time, as you already know how much better you feel for taking out so much of the garbage that has made up the majority of your food and drink consumption over the last few years. Whether you are restricted for time, money, or locally sourced fresh ingredients, you need to make a commitment to your own health and take responsibility for helping to make the improvements happen.

Kitchen equipment

We recommend that you equip your kitchen with all the right tools to make your life easier. You don't have to buy all this equipment in one go, but you do need to collect the essentials over time. Wait for sales to come up for the more expensive pieces (food processor, Vitamix blender, juicer) or check out eBay for those items that others have been given and simply never used. All this equipment is for your ease of preparation and can be hugely time-saving. A visit to a good kitchen store or catering outlet will inspire you to become your own chef-at-home!

- Food processor
- Vitamix blender (the best) or other good-quality, strong-blade blender
- Juicer (Braun, Waring, Phillips)
- Hand-held blender (great for soups and dips before you make a bigger investment)
- Mandolin
- Good set of knives
- Chopping boards
- Slow-cooker
- Dehydrator
- Spiralizer

STOCKING UP

The first important move is to make sure that you have all you need in your kitchen. Being prepared is the key!

Your stock of dry goods and herbs and spices is the foundation of a well-prepared healthy kitchen, allowing you to create a meal at the drop of a hat, with simply the addition of some fresh ingredients.

Include the following in your pantry and you will be able to create most of the recipes found in this book:

- Chickpeas, butter beans, black-eyed beans, pinto beans, red kidney beans
- Red and brown lentils, puy lentils, black beluga lentils, dhal red lentils, yellow split peas
- Pearl barley, brown rice, red Camargue rice, black rice noodles, buckwheat noodles
- Dried wakame, nori, and dulse seaweeds and bonito flakes
- Dried fruits for soaking in Bircher muesli—apricots, cranberries, goji berries, and raisins
- Cumin, turmeric, mustard seed, cinnamon, nutmeg, allspice, bay leaves, coriander seed, fenugreek seed, cumin seed, black and red peppercorns, paprika, cayenne pepper, sumac
- Agave syrup, manuka or raw honey, xylitol, yacon syrup
- Cashews, almonds, hazelnuts, pecans, walnuts (store in fridge for freshness)
- Almond nut, hazelnut, and cashew nut butters and tahini (should also be kept in fridge once opened or made)
- Coconut butter and coconut milk
- Cacao powder and cacao butter
- Apple cider vinegar, balsamic vinegar, Braggs Aminos, tamari (wheat-free soy sauce), mirin (rice wine)

Cooking methods for the Lifestyle

All the methods used in the Cleanse (see page 33) also apply to the Lifestyle phase of the program, with the inclusion of sautéing vegetables, tofu, and grains in the early part of their cooking. Sautéing allows oils to be used to cook the food at a lower temperature than frying, to soften the food, without overcooking or damaging the nutrients contained therein.

Healing herbs and spices

It's a good idea to choose recipes that use one, two, or more of these fantastic healing herbs and spices. You'll enjoy their benefits in no time.

Turmeric

Our number one favorite ingredient—*this ancient spice has been used in Ayurvedic medicine in India for over 3,000 years to boost the natural killer cells of the immune system, warding off infections, protecting against viruses, and may prevent the development of cancers.* Its yellow coloring is effected by the curcuminoids, an inherent healing compound in both turmeric and cumin, which are anti-inflammatory and stimulating to the liver and gall bladder in their natural detoxification processes.

Ginger

Also a favorite for us, we prefer to use fresh ginger, but dried ginger powder is also beneficial. This root vegetable also stimulates the liver to flush out toxins, helps with both morning and motion sickness, has been found to help lower cholesterol and high blood pressure, and is a marvellous tonic for the skin. *We love adding ginger to green smoothies, breads, salads, and main dishes to pep up the flavor and add a spring to your step.*

Chili peppers

Again, we encourage using fresh when you can, but wouldn't discourage dried chilies either. The heat of the chili comes from a compound called capsaicin, which is found in a lesser amount in bell peppers. *Capsaicin stimulates metabolism, supports thyroid function, helps curb carb cravings, and encourages good digestion and elimination.* Use carefully, and avoid at night if you are a light sleeper, as chilies will make you dream more vividly!

Garlic

Many of our dishes include garlic (both fresh and dried powdered), *as its healing properties are boundless —antibacterial, antiviral, anti-parasitic, and liver-supporting*, no healthy kitchen should be without garlic. The amino acid cysteine, which helps the liver in its detox processes, is the main healing component.

Sumac

Few people had heard of sumac until a few years ago, and yet it has been used for millennia to add spice and tartness to raw and cooked dishes, and is slightly sour to taste on its own. It is derived from a berry (*Rhus coriaria*), and grown in the Middle East and Italy. *Sumac stimulates the digestive enzymes in the mouth* (ptyalin) that help to break down dense proteins such as nuts, soy produce and beans, and legumes.

Mustard seeds

Rather than using mustard from a jar, which has vinegar, sugar, and sometimes additives, *the humble mustard seed has a lot to offer.* It adds fabulous flavor to salads and soups, while stimulating stomach acid production to ensure you digest your food more efficiently. It is also a rich source of selenium to boost metabolism and immunity.

Meal planning

We have provided you with over 100 recipes in this book to stimulate your palate and cooking skills. None of them are difficult to prepare and, in fact, you will be surprised by how quick and easy most of them are. However, we suggest you start with just two or three days' worth of recipes for breakfast, lunch, and dinner, with a couple of snacks, so as not to feel overwhelmed. On the contrary, once you have shopped for the ingredients for those days, you will have more confidence to incorporate this into your Lifestyle.

This is exactly how Natasha started, with her Fridge Fill service to her clients—supplying menus on a Sunday evening and cooking all the dishes on Monday to deliver for the next three days' worth of meals.

Start on a Sunday

If you are working full-time, we suggest you do all your shopping and cooking for the first three days on a Sunday, so that you don't have to think about what to cook for the first half of the week.

Remember that fresh food should be exactly that—*fresh*. Don't be tempted to bulk-buy fruit and vegetables unless you plan to bulk-cook and freeze portions of soups and casseroles! This is not a bad idea when you embark on the Lifestyle, so that you can stay "on program." However, you will soon see how satisfying, quick, and easy it is to prepare certain things daily, and we really encourage that all the fresh juices, smoothies, and salads are prepared at the time of consuming, for maximum benefit.

Snacking is positively encouraged

We have devoted a proportionately high amount of the recipes—both sweet and savory—to mini-meals and snacks, as this is an area where so many who are aiming to eat healthily fall down. Know that most commercially produced nut-and-seed bars are often

laden with sugar to prevent the bars from going rancid, and you will be far better off making your own (see Granola Bars, page 150, or Sticky Seed Granola Bars, page 152). Similarly, many commercial dips and spreads have high levels of salt and additives to prevent browning or rancidity. *When you see that it literally takes five minutes to prepare your own hummus (see Spinach and chickpea hummus, page 167) and you have plenty of celery, carrots, snow peas, and cucumbers in the fridge, you have ready-made alkaline snacks at your fingertips.* Even Avocado on Toast (see page 49) takes mere moments and is so satisfying, as the balance of protein to carbohydrates provides you with a perfect dose of slow-release energy.

Taking food when you travel

Whether you're traveling by road, rail, boat, or plane, the foods on offer at available cafés, bakeries, and delis are usually high-fat, high-sugar, high-salt, and therefore high-acid. This will simply leave you dehydrated, and yearning for more of the same.

Avoid these eventualities by being prepared—you can't take your own green juice on a plane, but you can take a bag of sprouted beans and seeds and those little pearls of protein will stave off hunger for hours! Similarly, if you know you have a car journey of several hours, bake some Coconut Bread (see page 160) or Chocolate Coconut Balls (see page 156), some Granola Bars (see page 150), or some dips and crudités (see pages 166–67), and make a batch of fresh vegetable juice to take in a thermos to preserve its freshness. *You will arrive at your destination perky and bright-eyed* as opposed to tired, irritable, and bloated!

Energy through the day

In a world where we are becoming increasingly overwhelmed and overburdened with our responsibilities, multitasking, and frequent travel, prioritizing *when* to eat is key. Too often, meals and snacks are "put off" in favor of "just finishing this before I eat." *In the Lifestyle, we encourage you to plan your day around when you eat, rather than the other way round.* In France and some other European countries, as well as China and Japan, large corporations have prioritized feeding their employees regularly

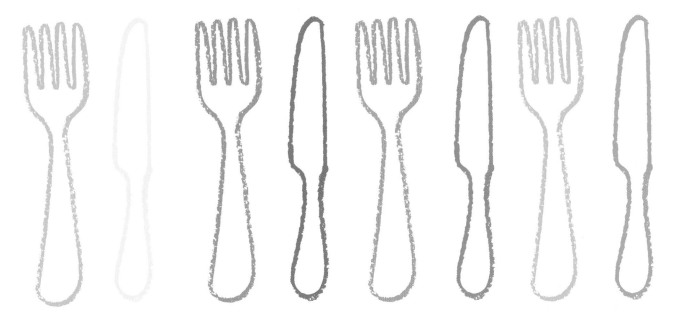

throughout the day as they know how this will affect productivity within the business. For many, especially those who work for themselves, this discipline simply isn't implemented. So, we recommend allocating a midday lunchtime, and start by setting an alarm on your watch or phone. *Moving away from your desk or other work station for half an hour at least to have a midday meal will more than double your productivity in the ensuing three hours.* Those who "skip" meals simply lower their productivity measurably. Additionally, if you are someone who works late into the evening, taking time for a late-afternoon high-protein snack (Beet and Walnut Dip, see page 166) or mini-meal (Falafel Wraps with salsa and yogurt, see page 70) ensures that your blood-sugar levels remain balanced, your concentration and focus sharp, and that the extra hours you put in are worth every minute.

Eating for exercise

Some like to exercise first thing in the morning, others at lunchtime, and the rest after work (or not at all!). As well as toning the body, exercise raises endorphins, which stimulate serotonin production—the "happy and contented" neurotransmitter that is received in both the brain, where it increases motivation, and the digestive system (sometimes known as the "second

brain"), where it produces feelings of calm and satisfaction. *It is no coincidence that the CEOs of both small and large businesses are the primary high-level exercisers.* They know the value of endorphins and serotonin production and of the feel-good factor and sense of being in control that goes with that.

Morning exercisers

If you are a runner and you choose to run in the morning, do not eat anything solid before you run—a good high-protein shake is what you need (see Smoothies, pages 46–48). Including soy or almond milk (see Milks, page 57), hemp or flax seed, almonds, cashews, and walnuts all add both protein and essential fats to your pre-workout drink. Anything more solid is likely to repeat on you when running. Post-run food should be eaten within half an hour and should be a good balance of protein, essential fats, and carbohydrate, for example Raw Buckwheat and Cinnamon Granola with fresh berries (see page 54).

Working out at lunchtime

If you exercise in your lunch hour, make sure to have a complex carbohydrate snack mid-morning, such as spelt or rye bread with a dip of your choice. This will ensure you have adequate glucose stores in the muscles to take you through your workout without leaving you feeling totally exhausted. Eating a well-balanced lunch mid-afternoon will balance your blood-sugar levels and ensure that you maintain focus and energy through the afternoon's work.

Exercising at the end of the day

For evening exercisers, you need a second mini-lunch (or more of the same from your first meal), to provide you with sufficient energy for your workout, and to prepare something satisfying for when you get home in the evening. *Soups provide a great balance of energy-fuelling complex carbohydrates and proteins; include pearl barley, quinoa, and buckwheat, with a vast array of seasonal vegetables to ensure ample antioxidants to mop up the free radicals produced in your workout.* You may either take a thermos flask with you to work, or know that you have a slow-cooked meal waiting for you when you get home.

For those who choose yoga as their primary form of exercise, remember that it is important not to eat for a couple of hours prior to your practice, as many of the asanas work directly on the digestive tract as a whole, and eating solid foods will cause discomfort. Drinking vegetable juices up to half an hour prior to your practice is preferable.

And for those who are not exercising at all—*get moving*! Lack of exercise is acid-forming in the body, promoting lack of energy and depression. Research has confirmed this fact time and again—hence the saying "eat with your body in mind," to which we always advocate moving your body. Lack of exercise leads to shallow breathing, which is also acid-forming, preventing the removal of natural toxins from the body. Whatever you choose to do, from dance to kick-boxing, running, riding, or swimming—just do it! Exercise is the number one stress-buster, and stress is the number one cause of disease.

Managing stress through food

It has been shown through much research that stress leads to increased production of cortisol, a hormone released from the adrenal glands in response to our "fight or flight" response mechanism in the body. Acute stress is manageable, and the adrenal glands have been designed to help rebalance our reaction to fright, surprise, shock, and immediate reactions for our survival. *However, chronic stress is depleting to the adrenals, and subsequently the thyroid gland (found at the base of the neck, just below your Adam's apple), as well as being highly acid-forming to the body.* This is why those who are under constant pressure at work, or caring for another family member constantly, or experiencing financial difficulties, regularly get sick. This is your body's way of telling you to take more care of yourself and prioritize your own health. This is a time when the alkaline approach is paramount, as your body is producing much acid, inflammation, and the precursors for serious disease. Think how often you have heard a friend saying, "I think I need to change my lifestyle—I can feel that there is something seriously wrong with me."

Don't wait for the seriously wrong to happen—take charge of your own health *now*, and embark on the Honestly Healthy program. You won't regret it, and you'll enjoy the benefits of feeling really well for the first time in years. Your energy will soar, your weight will balance itself to the weight you are supposed to be, and you will feel years younger within a matter of months.

We want you to have the benefits we have both found through living our lives this way—we know how easy it is to eat the alkaline way, because we do it ourselves. As they say, the proof of the pudding is in the eating, so get cooking in your kitchen and see for yourself. You can have the treats as well as all the greens, because we've made sure that they nourish you in the best way. *Eat with your body in mind.*

Menu Planner for the Lifestyle Phase

DAY 1
Morning
Nutty Granola with a nut milk
(pages 56–57)
Green Smoothie (pages 46–47)

Lunch
Spanish Omelet with Dill and Sweet
Potato (page 110) with a simple
green salad or Pulsed Fava Bean
and Pearl Barley Salad (page 99)

Snack
Beet and Walnut Dip
(page 166) with Raw Flax Seed
Crackers (page 167)

Evening
Thai Yellow Curry with Brown Rice
(page 142)

DAY 2
Morning
Scrambled Eggs and Portobello
Mushroom with Melted Goat's
Cheese (page 60)
Toxin Reducer juice (page 37)

Lunch
Sweetcorn and Fava Bean Fritters
with a Feta, Cucumber, and Spinach
Salad (pages 122–123)

Snack
Handful of almonds, soaked

Evening
Mixed Vegetable and Soybean
Hotpot (page 82) with Sweet
Potato Bread toast (page 162)

Dessert
Raw Chocolate Mousse (page 170)

DAY 3
Morning
Avocado on Toast (page 49)
Mango Coconut smoothie (page
48)

Lunch
Butternut Squash Soup (page 79)

Snack
Smoky Eggplant Dip (page 166)
with crudités

Evening
Caramelized Pear and Lentil Salad
(page 94)

DAY 4
Morning
Nut and Berry Layered Breakfast
(page 55)
Green Goddess juice (page 37)

Lunch
Quinoa and Cranberry Burgers
(page 116) with Pomegranate and
Mozzarella Salad (page 98)

Snack
"Cheesy" Kale Chips (page 159)

Evening
Red Rice and Beet Risotto
(page 130)
Sweet-potato Chocolate Brownie
(page 174)

DAY 5
Morning
Buckwheat Pancakes with
Blackberry Compote (page 52)

Lunch
Dill Steamed Artichoke (page 75)
with a serving of Roots and Walnut
Salad (page 98)

Snack
Spinach and Chickpea Hummus
(page 167) with raw crudités

Evening
Noodle and Smoked Tofu Salad
with Mirin Dressing (page 121)
Raw Mango Coconut Balls
(page 156)

breakfasts

Green Smoothies

A green smoothie isn't a juice, but a mixture of water, leafy greens, and fruits, thoroughly blended together. The blender breaks down the cellulose structure in the greens, thereby unlocking their valuable nutrients. You can change the fruit to whatever you like and add extra ingredients as you wish, so play around with flavors. Use about 40% greens to 60% fruit to start, plus just enough water to run the blender and create the thickness you like best. Smoothies are fast and easy to make and will complement any diet or lifestyle.

To make any of these smoothies, simply blend the ingredients in a Vitamix or high-speed blender until smooth. **All smoothies serve 2**

Fresh

♥ ♥ ♥ ⚘

1 ripe pear, cored and chopped
1 bunch of kale
Sprig of mint
1 cup purified or filtered water
1 cup apple juice

Hydrating Sweet Fix

♥ ♥ ⚘

1 soft ripe peach
1 banana
1¼ oz baby spinach leaves
1 tsp agave syrup
1 cup coconut water

Cold Buster

1 bunch of bok choy, roughly chopped
1 banana
Scant 1 cup frozen raspberries
Generous ¾ cup frozen blueberries
1⅓ cups purified or filtered water

Spicy

1 handful of spinach
Generous ¾ cup frozen blueberries
1 ripe pear, cored and chopped
½ ripe banana
1 tsp grated fresh ginger
1 cup purified or filtered water

THINGS TO ADD...
Probiotic powder
Omega oils (we love Udo's)
Raw flax seeds
Spirulina
Wheatgrass
Maca
Lúcuma (sweet-tasting)
Hemp protein powder
   (quite earthy-tasting, be warned)
Or add your "supergreens" powder
   instead of individually adding
   all the supergreens

The Ultimate Morning Wake-up

1 head of bok choy, roughly chopped
½ papaya
½ mango
½ cup purified or filtered water
1 cup coconut water
1 tbsp ground raw flax seeds
1 tsp spirulina powder or any
   "supergreens" powder
2 probiotic capsules (pull the capsule
   apart and tip out the contents)
1 tbsp Udo's oil

Skin Booster

4-in piece of cucumber,
   roughly chopped
1 handful of spinach
Juice of 1 lemon
2 celery stalks, roughly chopped
1 kiwi
¼ avocado
Scant 2 cups purified or filtered water

TIPS
• Coconut water can be added instead
  of water.
• Add agave syrup to sweeten if not
  quite sweet enough.

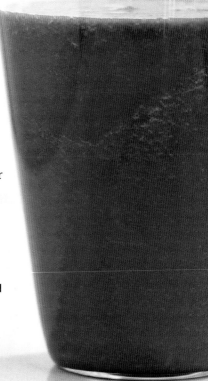

Fruit Smoothies

Nothing can beat these smoothies, complete with cholesterol-lowering fiber, energy-giving complex carbohydrates, and protein for building and repair.

Mango Coconut

⅓ mango, sliced
1 banana
Scant 2 cups coconut water
½ cup dry unsweetened shredded coconut
½ tsp vanilla extract

Very Berry

Generous ¾ cup mixed berries
Scant 1 cup raw almonds
1 ripe banana
⅛ tsp ground cinnamon
1–2 tbsp agave syrup (or a few drops of stevia), depending on the ripeness of the berries

Nutty Chocolate

Scant 2 cups Macadamia Nut Milk (see page 53)
2 very ripe bananas
2 tbsp raw unsweetened cacao powder
1 tsp vanilla extract
2 tbsp agave syrup, or to taste

Blueberry Nut

1 cup Hemp Milk (see page 57)
1 cup apple juice
2 bananas
1⅔ cups blueberries
Scant ¼ cup raw almonds
⅓ cup raw walnuts
2 tbsp raw flax seeds

Brazilian Berry

Scant 1 cup strawberries
Scant 1 cup raspberries
Generous ¾ cup blueberries
¼ cup raw Brazil nuts
3 cups purified or filtered water
2 ice cubes
3 ready-to-eat dried prunes
1 tbsp ground raw flax seeds
¼ tsp ground cinnamon

Blend the ingredients in a Vitamix or high-speed blender until smooth. **All smoothies serve 2**

Avocado on Toast

serves 1

1 ripe avocado

1 tbsp extra virgin olive oil

Juice of ½ lemon

1 slice of toast (made from
any of the bread recipes, see
pages 160–163)

Freshly ground black pepper

Super-quick and easy to make, and very nourishing and
filling to help you start the day. You can also have this
as a mid-afternoon snack to keep you going.

Remove the pit from the avocado and slice lengthwise into thin
slices. Gently toss the avocado slices in the olive oil and lemon juice.
Arrange the avocado slices on the toast. It's as simple as that.

Serve immediately, sprinkled with black pepper.

Not all fabulous treats need be bad for you—on the contrary, the macadamia nuts and pomegranate seeds help lower cholesterol, and quinoa is one of the highest protein seeds you can eat.

Buckwheat Pancakes

makes 6–8

½ cup buckwheat flour
½ cup rice flour
1 tsp baking powder
½ tsp Himalayan pink salt
Scant 1¼ cups Brown Rice Milk
    (see page 57)
1 tbsp lemon juice
1 tbsp sunflower oil, plus extra
    for greasing
1 tbsp rice syrup

(Pictured on page 50.) Feeling cozy and indulgent on a weekend? Why not treat yourself to a not-so-naughty breakfast. Feel free to experiment—try adding honey, stewed fruits, or even a delicious raw chocolate sauce!

Place the buckwheat flour, rice flour, baking powder, and salt in a large bowl and mix well.

Place the milk, lemon juice, sunflower oil, and rice syrup in another bowl and mix well, then stir into the dry ingredients and mix gently until just combined, being careful not to overmix.

Wipe a skillet lightly with oil and heat over medium heat. Place an egg ring or pastry ring in the pan and ladle in 1 tablespoon of the pancake mixture. Cook until air bubbles start to appear on the surface of the pancake. Do not turn until this point. Remove the mold, turn the pancake, and cook for about 1 minute on the other side, until set. Repeat until all the mixture is used and cooked.

Serve in a stack, layered with Blackberry Compote (see below) and soy yogurt, or with fresh fruit and agave syrup to accompany.

Blackberry Compote

Generous ¾ cup blackberries,
    rinsed and drained
2 tsp water
1 tbsp honey
Pancakes, granola, or yogurt, to
    serve

Place the ingredients in a pan over low heat. Simmer for 10 minutes, stirring occasionally, until the berries are lovely and soft.

Blend the compote until smooth and serve warm or chilled with pancakes, granola, or yogurt.

Quinoa Porridge with Macadamia Nut Milk

serves 4

Seeds from 1 pomegranate

2 cups quinoa flakes

Scant ⅔ cup goji berries

1 cinnamon stick

Scant 2 cups Macadamia Nut
   Milk (see below)

3 cups water

¾ cup raspberries

(Pictured on page 51.) Macadamia nuts, while more acidic in pH, have abundant essential fats and zinc to boost immunity, while goji berries add the antioxidant beta-carotene. This "porridge" is higher in protein than the conventional hot cereal made with oats.

To remove the seeds from the pomegranate, roll it firmly on a work surface to loosen the seeds, then cut it in half and scoop out the seeds with a teaspoon (or see page 98 for another method). Set aside while you make the oatmeal.

Place the quinoa flakes, goji berries, cinnamon stick, 1 cup of the macadamia nut milk, and scant 2 cups of the water in a pan. Stir continuously over medium heat for 2–3 minutes, then crush the raspberries into the pan, add the remaining water, and stir for another 2 minutes, until piping hot.

Heat the remaining macadamia milk in a separate pan.

Spoon the oatmeal into 4 bowls, pour over the hot macadamia milk, and serve sprinkled with the pomegranate seeds.

Macadamia Nut Milk

1⅓ cups raw macadamia nuts,
   soaked for about 4 hours and
   drained

3–4 cups purified or filtered
   water

Blend the ingredients in a Vitamix or high-speed blender until smooth, then filter through a cheesecloth bag or a very fine strainer.

Store for up to 2 days in the fridge in a glass jar with an airtight lid.

Raw Buckwheat and Cinnamon Granola

Buckwheat is a great source of rutin, helping to strengthen the capillaries and veins throughout the body, supporting the cardiovascular system, and helping to prevent thread and varicose veins in the legs.

Soak the buckwheat overnight in cold water, then rinse well (the discarded soaking water will be slimy and gelatinous), cover with fresh water, and leave to soak and plump up for another day. Rinse again and drain well. Alternatively, bring the buckwheat to a boil, then simmer over low heat for 15 minutes. Rinse in cold water, drain well, and proceed with the recipe as follows.

Place all the ingredients in a bowl and mix well, then spread them in a thin layer on a dehydrator sheet and place in the dehydrator at 105–110°F for 10 hours.

Alternatively, spread the mixture in a thin layer on a baking sheet and either place in the oven at the lowest temperature with the door open for 10 hours, or bake in a preheated oven at 225°F for 1 hour.

Let the mixture cool completely before serving with yogurt or dairy-free milk and fresh fruit.

serves 2
♥♥♥

Generous ¾ cup raw buckwheat groats
½ cup raw almonds, soaked overnight and drained
½ cup mixed raw pumpkin, sunflower, and flax seeds
1 tsp ground cinnamon
Scant ½ cup mixed raisins and chopped dried figs
3 tbsp agave syrup
1 tbsp dry unsweetened shredded coconut

To serve
Yogurt or a dairy-free milk (see pages 53 and 57)
Fresh fruit of your choice

NUTRITIONAL NUGGET
Cinnamon is a potent anti-inflammatory, helping to settle bloating, wind, and general abdominal discomfort.

Nut and Berry Layered Breakfast

serves 2–4

1 cup raw walnuts
Scant ⅔ cup raw almonds
⅓ cup raw pumpkin seeds
Scant ⅓ cup raw sunflower
   seeds
⅓ cup raw flax seeds
1 large punnet of blueberries
1 large punnet of raspberries
1 quantity of Raw Vanilla
   Cashew Cream (see below)

Keep your pantry well stocked with nuts and seeds so you can throw this yummy breakfast together in minutes (remember to allow time for soaking).

Soak all the nuts and seeds for 30 minutes to 1 hour and drain. Then tip them into a food processor and pulse briefly—just enough to coarsely chop, but still retain their wonderful crunchy texture.

To serve, place a layer of berries in the bottom of a glass, place a layer of nut mix on top, and spoon over a layer of the Raw Vanilla Cashew Cream. Repeat the layers and decorate with berries. Repeat to make the number of servings you require.

Raw Vanilla Cashew Cream

⅔ cup raw cashews, soaked for
   1 hour and drained
¼–½ cup purified or filtered
   water
1 tsp vanilla extract

Drain the nuts and put in a blender. Add ¼ cup of the water and blend, adding more water as necessary to make a smooth cream, then add the vanilla extract and blend for a few more seconds.

Nutty Granola

serves 4

Generous ¼ cup dried dates

Generous 1 cup jumbo rolled
   oats

2 tbsp honey

½ cup mixed raw cashews and
   pecans

1¾ tbsp raw pumpkin seeds

3 tbsp olive oil

This is simply amazing. Make a batch and store in an airtight glass container and use it as a breakfast cereal or a crunchy topping on yogurt or oatmeal.

Preheat the oven to 325°F.

Simmer the dates in ½ in water until soft and then blend until smooth. Stir in the remaining ingredients and mix well.

Spread the mixture on a baking sheet and bake for 15 minutes until golden, then reduce the oven temperature to 225°F and bake for another 30 minutes or until the mixture is dry and crisp.

Let cool completely, then store in an airtight container.

Milks

These milks are well worth the planning, although they don't take that much effort to make. They are all excellent alternatives to dairy milk.

Almond Milk

Scant 1 cup raw almonds, soaked for
   4 hours and drained
3–4 cups purified or filtered water

Brown Rice Milk

¾ cup cooked brown rice, soaked for
   4 hours before cooking
Scant 2 cups purified or filtered water

Hemp Milk

Scant 1¼ cups shelled hemp seeds,
   soaked for 4 hours and drained
5 cups purified or filtered water

Brazil Nut Milk

¾ cup raw Brazil nuts, soaked for
   4 hours and drained
3–4 cups purified or filtered water

To make any milk, simply blend the ingredients in a Vitamix or high-speed blender until smooth, then filter through a cheesecloth bag or a very fine strainer. Store for up to 2 days in the fridge in a glass jar with an airtight lid.

The Full Breakfast

serves 2

6 asparagus spears, trimmed

1 stem of vine-ripened baby
   tomatoes, divided into 2

2 portobello mushrooms, sliced

1 small garlic clove, sliced

1½ tsp olive oil

¼ cup hard goat's cheese,
   grated

4 eggs

7 oz spinach

Juice of ½ lemon

Freshly ground black pepper

Gluten-/wheat-free bread, to
   serve (optional)

NUTRITIONAL NUGGET
Eggs are a source of the essential
nutrient choline—vital for a
healthy brain and smart thinking.

Who said a substantial breakfast need be greasy and fattening? Not in our book! This is perfect for a Sunday brunch or even a scruffy supper. You can play with the recipe—scramble or boil the eggs, and add whatever is in the fridge.

Preheat the oven to 350°F.

Place the asparagus, tomatoes on their vines, and the mushrooms with garlic on top on a baking sheet, drizzle with a teaspoon of the olive oil, and bake for 20 minutes (cherry tomatoes work well, too, but they'll need a bit less time, just till the skins split).

Remove from the oven and sprinkle the grated goat's cheese on the mushrooms and allow to melt.

Meanwhile, fill a skillet with water to within 1 in of the top, bring to a boil, then reduce the heat to a simmer. When the asparagus and mushrooms have been in the oven for 15 minutes, crack the eggs very carefully into the simmering water and poach for 3 minutes, making sure that the water completely covers the eggs—if necessary, spoon the cooking water over the eggs while they cook.

Place the spinach in a bowl, cover with boiling water, and let stand for 2 minutes, then drain well and add the remaining olive oil and the lemon juice. Divide between 2 serving plates.

Carefully remove the eggs from the water with a slotted spoon and arrange on the spinach. Place some mushrooms on each plate with the asparagus and the vine tomatoes. Sprinkle with black pepper.

Serve immediately, with a piece of gluten-/wheat-free bread, if liked.

Scrambled Eggs and Baked Portobello Mushroom with Melted Goat's Cheese

serves 1

1 large portobello mushroom

1 tbsp olive oil

Pinch of Himalayan pink salt

¾ oz hard goat's cheese, sliced

2 eggs

1 egg yolk

2 tbsp finely chopped dill, plus extra for garnishing (optional)

Scrambling eggs takes only minutes—but, remember, to make them oh-so-creamy cook over a low, low heat and stir constantly. By adding different herb combinations, you can make this dish your own.

Preheat the oven to 340°F.

Place the mushroom on a baking sheet, drizzle with the olive oil, and sprinkle with a pinch of salt. Bake for 15 minutes, then arrange the goat's cheese slices on top and return to the oven for 3 minutes to melt the cheese.

Beat the whole eggs and egg yolk in a bowl and add the dill, then pour them into a hot pan and cook over low heat, stirring constantly, to the consistency you require.

Serve immediately with the mushroom and goat's cheese, with a little extra chopped dill if you like.

NUTRITIONAL NUGGET

All mushrooms are a fantastic source of vitamin D, which most of us lack if we are not living in sunny climates—so stock up in the winter on this sunshine food.

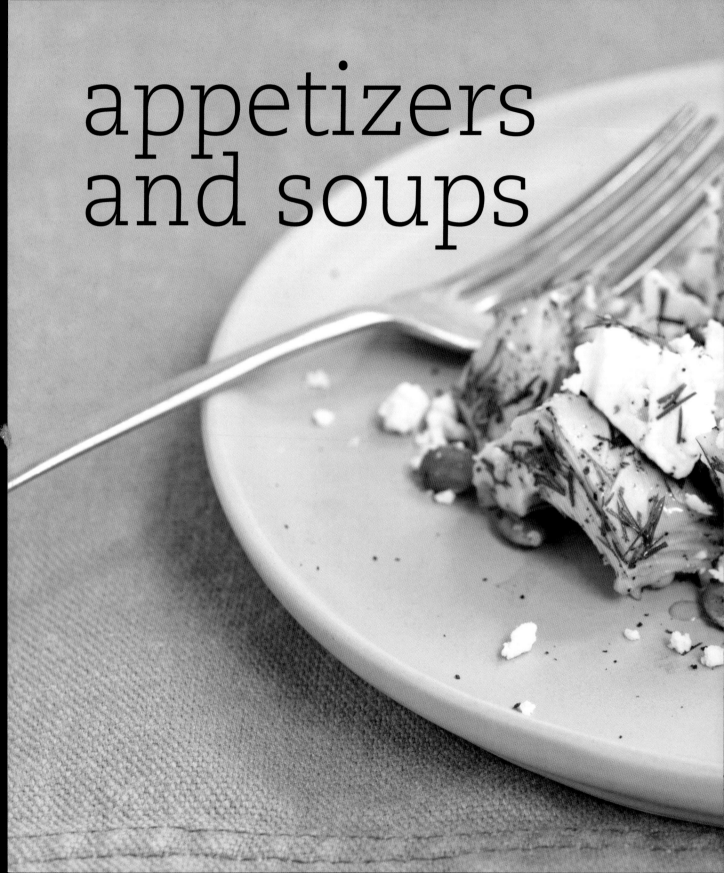

appetizers and soups

Artichoke Hearts with Feta

serves 2

7 oz canned artichoke hearts,
  chopped

2 tsp extra virgin olive oil

Juice of 1 lemon

¼ cup feta, diced

2 tbsp raw pumpkin seeds

To serve

Pinch of sumac

2 tbsp finely chopped dill

(Pictured on pages 62–63) This takes moments to prepare. We've used canned artichoke hearts but you could try roasted Jerusalem artichokes for a different flavor.

Mix the artichoke hearts with the olive oil and lemon juice in a bowl, then gently fold in the feta and pumpkin seeds.

Serve garnished with sumac and chopped dill.

Cashew Dipping Sauce for Raw Summer Spring Rolls

½ cup raw cashews, soaked
  and drained

2 oz cucumber, peeled and
  chopped

½ small red bell pepper,
  deseeded and chopped

1 small garlic clove

2 red chilies, deseeded

Dash or two of tamari sauce,
  to taste

Squeeze of lime juice

Squeeze of agave syrup

Place all the ingredients in a blender and process briefly, then add water a little at a time, processing after each addition to make a smooth and creamy sauce.

Transfer to a small bowl and serve as a dipping sauce.

NUTRITIONAL NUGGET
Cashew nuts are a fantastic source of niacin—a B vitamin known to elevate mood! A handful of cashews is a natural alternative to Prozac.

Raw Summer Spring Rolls

serves 2

4 rice paper rounds

1 nori seaweed sheet, cut into
  4 squares

1 carrot, cut into julienne strips

1 zucchini, cut into julienne
  strips

1 scallion, cut into fine strips

1 small cucumber, cut into
  julienne strips

Chunk of Napa cabbage,
  shredded

1 packet bean sprouts

1 handful of cilantro, chopped

Scant ½ cup smoked tofu,
  diced

Practice makes perfect with these little parcels. At first
it's a little fiddly but you'll get the hang of it in no time.
The trick here is not to oversoak the rice paper rounds.

Soak the rice paper rounds in cold water for about 1 minute to just
soften them, then remove from the water and pat dry. Lay each rice
paper round on a flat surface and place a nori square on top of each.

Arrange a medley of vegetables, tofu, and cilantro in the center of
each paper/nori wrapper. Roll the edge nearest to you over the filling
and then tuck in the outside edges. Continue to roll carefully but
tightly. This does take a little practice, but delicate handling will get
you there in a short time.

Serve alongside the Cashew Dipping Sauce (see opposite) and
perhaps some watercress or salad greens.

Stuffed Round Zucchini

serves 2

2 small round zucchini

1 tsp olive oil

3 garlic cloves

1 small onion, finely chopped

2 oz carrot, finely grated

1 tsp thyme leaves

1 tsp oregano leaves

2 canned artichoke hearts,
   chopped

½ tsp grated lemon zest

½ tsp Himalayan pink salt

Scant ¼ cup raw cashews,
   chopped

1 oz feta, crumbled

To serve

Arugula leaves

Cherry tomatoes

Radish sprouts

Extra virgin olive oil,
   for drizzling

Beautiful to present for a dinner party as an appetizer or even as your main course, served with brown rice and a crunchy salad. If you are vegan, just leave out the feta as the cashews provide plenty of protein.

Preheat the oven to 300°F. Next, trim the stalks off the zucchini. Brush a roasting pan with ½ teaspoon of the olive oil, add the zucchini and garlic, and roast for 50 minutes, until tender. Remove from the oven, leaving the oven on. When the zucchini are cool enough to handle, carefully scoop out the flesh and set aside.

Heat the remaining oil in a pan and gently sauté the onion for 5 minutes. Add the carrot, thyme, and oregano and sauté for another 5 minutes, or until the carrot is soft. Add the zucchini flesh and chopped artichoke hearts and sauté for 2 minutes.

Stir in the lemon zest, salt, and chopped cashews. Divide the mixture between the zucchini shells, stuffing it in tightly. Top with the crumbled feta and return to the oven for 15–20 minutes or until the feta is golden.

Serve the zucchini with the Fig Jam (see below) and a simple salad of arugula leaves, cherry tomatoes, and peppery radish sprouts, drizzled with a good olive oil.

Fig Jam

3½ oz figs

2 tsp balsamic vinegar

1 tsp rice syrup

1 tbsp water

While the zucchini are in the oven, chop the figs and place in a pan with the balsamic vinegar, rice syrup, and water. Simmer gently until the figs become soft and sticky.

Bok Choy Parcels

makes 6

2 tsp toasted sesame oil

3¼ oz eggplant, cut into
    julienne strips

2 garlic cloves, minced

1 tbsp water

2¾ oz carrot, grated

1¾ oz water chestnuts, cut into
    julienne strips

1¾ tbsp mixed raw black and
    white sesame seeds, toasted

½ tsp tamari

1 tsp white miso paste

¾ oz dried sliced mushrooms,
    soaked in hot water until
    softened

6 outer bok choy leaves

Sprouts, to garnish

These beautiful parcels are totally divine. A little bit fiddly to construct, but once you bite into them they just explode with flavor in your mouth.

First, make the Black Bean Sauce (see below). To make the filling for the parcels, heat a skillet and add the sesame oil. Add the eggplant and garlic and sauté for 2 minutes. Stir in the water, then add the carrot and water chestnuts and stir-steam ("fry" with water to create steam to sweat the vegetables) for another 5 minutes, until softened. Mix in the sesame seeds and tamari, then transfer the filling to a bowl and set aside.

Return the pan to the heat and add the miso paste and a splash of water. Spread the miso around the pan to heat through, then return the filling to the pan with the mushrooms and stir well.

To assemble the parcels, steam the bok choy leaves for 3–5 minutes, until just tender. Trim off the stalks, leaving a little to keep the leaf intact. Place the leaf on a board with the stem end facing you. Place a spoonful of the filling in the center of the leaf at the stem end, then roll the stem end over the filling, fold in the sides, and very carefully roll up the parcel so the filling is securely enclosed.

Serve immediately with the Black Bean Sauce or refrigerate and steam for 2 minutes just before serving and garnish with sprouts.

Black Bean Sauce

1 tsp light sesame oil

Scant ⅔ cup Chinese fermented
    black beans

1 garlic clove, minced

2 tsp grated fresh ginger

½ tsp oregano

½ tsp ground cumin

¼ tsp grated orange zest

Generous ⅓ cup water

1 tbsp rice vinegar

½ tbsp tamari

1 tsp agave syrup

To make the sauce, heat the sesame oil in a pan over medium-high heat. Add the beans and garlic and stir for 1 minute, then add the remaining ingredients and stir until the sauce thickens.

Falafel Wraps

serves 2

Scant ½ cup ground raw flax
   seeds
⅓ cup raw sesame seeds
2 carrots, peeled and thinly
   sliced
2 portobello mushrooms, diced
½ small onion, finely chopped
1 garlic clove, finely chopped
3 tbsp olive oil
Pinch of Himalayan pink salt
1 cup pistachios
Generous ¾ cup raw almonds
Scant 1 cup raw sunflower
   seeds, soaked for 30 minutes
   and drained
1 tbsp finely chopped parsley
¾ tsp ground cumin
1 tsp lemon juice
Freshly ground black pepper

To serve (see opposite)
Iceberg Lettuce Wraps
Mint Yogurt
Tomato Salsa

Cooking a variety of seeds, like this, at a very low temperature in the oven protects the essential fats that they provide and ensures that the flavor remains fresh and the taste crunchy.

Preheat the oven to 225°F.

Combine the ground flax seeds and sesame seeds in a bowl and set aside.

Combine the carrots, mushrooms, onion, garlic, and 2 tablespoons of the olive oil in a separate bowl. Add a pinch of salt and mix well. Place the pistachios, almonds, and sunflower seeds in a food processor and process to a crumbly texture. Add the nut mixture to the vegetable mixture, together with the parsley, cumin, and lemon juice. Mix thoroughly and season to taste with black pe,pper.

Form the mixture into balls 1¼–1¾ in in diameter. Roll the falafel balls in the flax- and sesame-seed mix to coat well. Place on a baking sheet and bake for about 40 minutes, or until crisp on the outside but still moist.

Serve the falafels, lettuce wraps, tomato salsa, and mint yogurt in separate bowls. To assemble, place 3 falafels in a lettuce wrap and add a spoonful each of tomato salsa and mint yogurt.

For the Iceburg Lettuce Wraps
1 head of iceberg lettuce

Chop the root off the lettuce and carefully peel away the large outer leaves. Place them in a large bowl of cold water until you are ready to serve, to keep them crisp and fresh. Pat dry to use.

Mint Yogurt

Scant 1 cup soy yogurt
1 oz mint leaves

Place the yogurt in a bowl. Just before serving, finely chop the mint and stir into the yogurt (don't chop before you are ready as the mint will turn black).

Tomato Salsa

2¼ cups tomatoes, finely diced
½ cup red onion, finely diced
1 small cucumber, deseeded
    and finely diced
1 red chili, deseeded and finely
    diced
½ garlic clove, grated
2 tbsp olive oil
Juice of 1 lime

Place all the ingredients in a bowl and mix gently to combine.

Stuffed New Potatoes

makes 10/serves 2

5 new potatoes

2 tbsp olive oil, plus extra for
   brushing

Pinch of Himalayan pink salt

Pinch of ground cumin

4 oz canned artichoke hearts

½ cup cooked cannellini beans

Juice of 1 lemon

1 tsp sumac, plus extra to
   garnish

Preheat the oven to 340°F.

Put the potatoes in an ovenproof dish, brush with olive oil, and sprinkle with the salt. Bake for 45 minutes, or until tender. Remove from the oven and let cool for 15 minutes, leaving the oven on.

When the potatoes are cool enough to handle, cut each one in half and carefully scoop out and discard the flesh (this can be mashed or used in soup). Place the scooped-out skins on a baking sheet, sprinkle with cumin, then return to the oven for another 15 minutes until crisp and golden. Set aside to cool.

To make the dip, process the remaining ingredients in a blender.

Serve the potato skins filled with the bean dip, garnished with a sprinkle of sumac.

Baby Yellow Squash Canapés

makes 8/serves 2

6 dried porcini mushrooms

8 baby yellow squash

1 tbsp olive oil

1 garlic clove, chopped

¼ cup curly kale (thick stems
   removed), roughly chopped

3 tbsp finely chopped parsley

1 large beefsteak tomato,
   deseeded and finely diced

1 tbsp soft goat's cheese

Soak the mushrooms in hot water for 30 minutes, drain on paper towel for 2 minutes, then dice.

Preheat the oven to 340°F. Place the baby yellow squash on a baking sheet and bake for 20 minutes, or until the skins are soft and slightly wrinkled. Remove and set aside to cool.

Meanwhile, heat the olive oil in a pan over low heat and gently sauté the garlic for 1 minute. Add the diced soaked mushroom, kale, and parsley and stir continuously for another 1 minute. Add the diced tomato and stir for another 2 minutes, then remove from the heat.

When the squash are cool enough to handle, cut off the tops with a small knife and carefully scoop out the flesh with a teaspoon, leaving a ¼-in shell and keeping the skin intact.

Just before serving, add the goat's cheese to the mushroom, kale, and tomato mixture, and heat through to melt the cheese. Stuff the baby yellow squash with the filling and serve warm.

These mini-squash canapés are super-healthy, antioxidant-packed morsels that can be eaten with glee —kale is rich in iron and calcium, while baby yellow squash are packed with beta-carotene to ward off environmental damage to the skin.

Eggplant and Pesto Rolls

makes 6 rolls/serves 2

4 oz eggplant
3 tbsp olive oil
Scant ¼ cup pine nuts
¼ oz flat-leaf parsley
1 small garlic clove
¾ oz feta, crumbled
Scant 1½ cups arugula leaves

These little beauties are so delicious and versatile. You could serve these appetizers on a platter at a party or team with a vibrant salad for a simple supper for two.

Preheat the oven to 340°F.

Slice the eggplant lengthwise into 6 x ¼-in slices. Place on a baking sheet lined with baking parchment, drizzle with 1 tablespoon of the olive oil, and bake in the oven for 15 minutes, or until tender. Set aside to cool.

Meanwhile, whiz the pine nuts, parsley, garlic, and remaining olive oil to a rough paste in a blender.

Divide the pesto between the eggplant slices and spread it down the center. Top each one with the feta, roll up the eggplant slices, and secure with toothpicks.

To serve, arrange the arugula on 2 plates and top with 3 rolls.

Dill Steamed Artichokes

You cannot beat the satisfaction of eating a globe artichoke—it's a meal in itself—or serve it as an appetizer for a dinner party.

serves 1

1 artichoke
1 tbsp olive oil
1 garlic clove
3 tbsp finely chopped dill
Scant 1 cup purifed or filtered
   water

For the dressing

2 tbsp tamari
1 tbsp balsamic vinegar
2 tbsp olive oil
1 tbsp agave syrup

Chop the long stem off the artichoke, leaving just a short one.

Heat the olive oil in a very deep pan, then gently sauté the garlic for 1 minute. Stir in 2 tablespoons of the chopped dill.

Add the water and then the artichoke, stem pointing upward. Cover the pan and steam over a low heat for 45-55 minutes, topping up with water when necessary. The artichoke is cooked when you can pull the leaves out easily and the "flesh" is tender.

Meanwhile, whisk together all the dressing ingredients.

Serve the artichoke sprinkled with the remaining chopped dill and accompanied with the dressing in a pot on the side.

Do as the Chinese do, "warm your body's cooker" by starting your meal with a soup. If you want to eat mainly raw in the winter, make sure you have either a small bowl of soup or a glass of hot water prior to your raw meal, as this helps to digest your food more effectively.

Vegetable and Quinoa Warming Soup

serves 2

⅓ cup quinoa

1½ tsp bouillon powder

Scant 1 cup purified or filtered
water

6 broccolini stalks, chopped

3½ oz leeks, chopped

Juice of 2 limes

2 tsp tamari

⅓ cup tofu, cubed

4 tbsp finely chopped cilantro,
to garnish (optional)

(Pictured on page 76.) This gentle, warming soup is a great addition to your repertoire. You can add whatever vegetables you have in your refrigerator—it's a staple request in my house on a Sunday night!

Measure the volume of the quinoa and bring twice the volume of water to a boil in a pan. Add the quinoa and the bouillon powder, bring back to a boil, then simmer for 5 minutes.

Boil the measured water and add to the pan with the broccolini and leeks, lime juice, and tamari and simmer for another 5 minutes.

Add the tofu and simmer for another 2 minutes, until the tofu is heated through.

Serve garnished with chopped cilantro, if wished.

NUTRITIONAL NUGGET
Did you know that soaking your nuts and seeds at least 2 hours before eating re-activates the enzymes into a "live" food, that is easier to digest, making your snack, meal, or juice super-nutritious?

Butternut Squash Soup

serves 4

3 tbsp olive oil

1 red onion, chopped

1 large garlic clove, chopped

2½ cups purified or filtered
water

1½ lb butternut squash, peeled,
deseeded, and chopped

1 large carrot, chopped

1 tsp bouillon powder

1 red chili, deseeded and
chopped

½ tsp finely grated fresh
ginger

1 tsp lemon juice

**For the cilantro and
parsley oil**

Leaves from ½ small bunch of
cilantro, finely chopped

Leaves from ½ small bunch
of flat-leaf parsley, finely
chopped

6 tbsp olive oil

Pinch of ground cumin

(Pictured on page 77.) I love making soups—they are so delicious. If you make batches and freeze them in portions, all you have to do is simply defrost and reheat —so you always have a tasty, nutritious meal at hand.

Heat the olive oil in a large pan, add the onion and garlic, and sauté gently for 5 minutes until softened, then add 5 teaspoons of the water and continue cooking until the onion absorbs the water.

Add the butternut squash and carrot and cook gently until they start to sweat. Add the remaining water and the bouillon powder, bring to a boil, and simmer for 15 minutes.

Next, put the red chili, ginger, and lemon juice in the pan and simmer for another 15 minutes.

Meanwhile, to make the herb oil, stir the chopped herbs into the oil with a pinch of cumin. Alternatively, whiz the whole leaves with the oil and cumin in a mini food processor until finely chopped.

Transfer the soup to a blender (or use a hand-held blender in the pan) and blend until smooth. Serve hot, drizzled with the cilantro and parsley oil.

TIP

By simmering the ingredients over low heat with splashes of water you start to layer the flavors, which really helps to bring out the subtle hits of each ingredient. The drizzle of herb oil is a perfect garnish.

Fennel and Pear Soup

serves 2

1 large fennel bulb, trimmed

1 tbsp olive oil, plus extra for drizzling

1 onion, sliced

1 garlic clove, chopped

2½ cups vegetable stock (made with ½ tsp bouillon powder)

1 pear, cored and chopped

NUTRITIONAL NUGGET
Fennel provides good support to the liver for cleansing, while both pear and fennel are packed with potassium, the most alkalizing of all the minerals. Potassium also helps regulate fluid retention in the body, ensuring that all nutrients are delivered to where they are needed, and preventing any possibility of dehydration at a cellular level.

This fabulous soup is one of my favorites. Both pear and fennel are high in pectin, which help to draw toxins out of the body, so this is a perfect candidate for the Cleanse or Lifestyle phases. Its rich flavors and creaminess are absolutely delicious and you just won't believe that there is no naughtiness in it!

Slice the fennel bulb in half, then, using a very sharp knife, cut 4 thin slivers and set aside, covered, to use as a garnish. Chop the remaining fennel.

Heat the olive oil in a large pan and sauté the onion and garlic, adding 3 tablespoons of the stock when they start to dry out.

Add the chopped fennel, adding another 3 tablespoons of the vegetable stock when this starts to dry out. Add the pear and the remaining stock, bring to a boil, then simmer for 40 minutes, until the fennel is wonderfully tender.

Transfer the vegetables and pear to a blender (or use a hand-held blender in the pan) with some of the liquid and blend until smooth, adding as much of the remaining liquid as necessary to make the exact consistency you like.

Serve garnished with the reserved fennel and a swirl of olive oil.

WHAT IS BOUILLON POWDER?
Made only from vegetables, this stock powder gives you instant stock whenever you need it or a touch of saltiness if that's what's called for.

Mixed Vegetable and Soybean Hotpot

serves 4

2 tsp soybean paste

3²/₃ cups purified or filtered
    water

2 sprigs of lemon thyme

½ onion, diced

3½ oz carrots, cubed

3½ oz potatoes, cubed

3½ oz pumpkin, cubed

3½ oz zucchini, cubed

3½ oz mixed red and yellow
    bell peppers, deseeded and
    cubed

3½ oz firm tofu, cubed

Simple, easy, and clean is the motto for this little bowl of broth packed with vegetable goodness. It takes less than half an hour to make, perfect after a long day.

Dissolve the soybean paste in the water in a large pan. Bring to a boil, add the lemon thyme sprigs, then simmer for 3–4 minutes to infuse the broth. Discard the lemon thyme sprigs.

Add the onion, carrots, and potatoes and cook for 10 minutes. Add the pumpkin, zucchini, and bell peppers and cook for another 5–10 minutes, or until the vegetables are just tender.

Add the tofu and simmer for another 2 minutes.

Serve immediately in warmed bowls and garnish with cilantro and sliced scallions, if wished.

NUTRITIONAL NUGGET

Tofu is a great source of vegetarian protein but we suggest you limit using soy products to three times a week as the phytoestrogens are potent.

If you shut your eyes and slurp away at this soup, you transport yourself to Thailand—these creamy coconut and lemongrass flavors really whisk you away to a beach when it's cold outside!

Tomato, Coconut, and Chili Soup

serves 2

1 tbsp coconut oil
½ cup shallots, chopped
¾ oz fresh ginger, chopped
1 garlic clove, chopped
½ red chili, chopped
1 lemongrass stalk, chopped
1 tsp coriander seeds
Scant 2 cups tomatoes, chopped

1²/₃ cups coconut milk
1 tsp tamari
1 tsp lime juice

To serve
Coconut cream
Chili oil
Finely chopped cilantro (optional)

Heat the coconut oil in a large pan. Add the shallots, ginger, and garlic and sauté gently for 5 minutes, until softened. Add the chili, lemongrass, and coriander seeds and sauté for another 5 minutes. Add the chopped tomatoes and sauté for another 5 minutes.

Stir in the coconut milk, bring to a boil, then simmer for 30 minutes. Season with tamari and a little lime juice.

Transfer the soup to a blender (or use a hand-held blender in the pan) and blend until smooth. Pass through a fine sieve if you want it even smoother.

Serve hot, garnished with a swirl of coconut cream, a drizzle of chili oil, and, if you like, a sprinkle of chopped fresh cilantro.

White Gazpacho

This is a super-easy recipe. Almonds are the most alkaline of all nuts, and rich in magnesium to help you relax and sleep well. Add a swirl of olive oil to each bowl for added essential fats.

serves 4

2 cups canned cannellini beans

2 cups canned butter beans

Scant 1 cup raw almonds

Scant 2 cups purified or filtered water

1 handful of mint

2 small cucumbers, peeled and chopped

Scant 1 cup apple juice

1 tsp extra virgin olive oil, plus extra to garnish

Zest and juice of 1 lemon

1 red chili, deseeded

1 handful of ice

First, rinse the canned beans and drain. Place the almonds, beans, and water in a blender and blend until smooth, then add all the remaining ingredients, except the ice.

Just before serving, blend in the ice, then serve immediately, garnished with a swirl of olive oil and some strips of lemon zest, chili, and mint.

TIP

This is a variation on a classic Spanish soup that has been used for years to boost immunity and relieve digestive complaints.

salads

Watercress, Roasted Onion, and Pistachio Salad

serves 1

♥ ♥ ♥ �’

½ red onion, cut into chunks

1 tbsp olive oil

Generous ⅛ cup canned chickpeas, rinsed and drained

1 small garlic clove, finely grated

½ red chili, finely sliced diagonally

½ oz deseeded cucumber, finely sliced

2 tbsp raw pumpkin seeds

2 tbsp raw pistachios

2¾ oz watercress

1 scallion, sliced diagonally

For the dressing

2 tbsp olive oil

Juice of 1 lemon

1 tbsp tamari

1 tsp agave syrup

(Pictured on pages 86–87.) This salad is a show-stopper —I love to make a big platter, put it in the middle of the table, and let people serve themselves, but it also makes a great supper for one if you are having a quiet night in.

Preheat the oven to 340°F.

Place the onion chunks on a baking sheet, drizzle with the olive oil, and bake for 30 minutes, or until soft.

Place the chickpeas in a bowl with the roasted onion and the garlic and mix thoroughly. Stir in the chili, cucumber, pumpkin seeds, and pistachios.

Whisk the dressing ingredients together with a fork.

To serve, scatter the watercress on a plate, top with the chickpea mixture, scallion, and drizzle over the dressing.

TIP
You could also try caramelizing your onions in balsamic vinegar and agave for a sweeter, not-so-naughty taste! (Follow the method for caramelizing pears on page 94.)

Avocado, Mango, and Dill Salad

serves 1

1¼ oz baby spinach leaves
1 tbsp olive oil
Pinch of sumac
Juice of 1 lime
¼ ripe avocado, diced
3½ oz mango, diced
¼ oz dill, chopped into
    ½-in pieces
1 small garlic clove, grated
1-in piece of red chili, finely
    sliced diagonally,
    to garnish
Sprouts, to garnish

You just can't beat a summer salad! This is delicious and doesn't leave you feeling at all bloated—ideal for those spring and summer months when you are wearing slightly lighter clothes!

Toss the baby spinach leaves with the olive oil, sumac, and lime juice and arrange in a bowl.

Place the avocado and mango, most of the dill, and the garlic in a separate bowl and mix together. Spoon onto the spinach and serve immediately, garnished with the chili, sprouts, and the remaining dill.

"Quick and delish" is the motto for these two dishes. They were created when in a rush and starving at the end of a long day, but I have also served both salads at a dinner party and the guests loved them!

Fennel and Halloumi Salad

serves 2

1 cup fennel, finely sliced

Juice of ½ lemon

2 tbsp olive oil

Scant ½ cup sheep's halloumi
cheese, diced

1 small garlic clove, grated

Scant ½ cup dried cranberries,
soaked in warm water for 20
minutes and drained

½ oz dill, chopped

(Pictured on page 90.) Halloumi—or "squeaky cheese" (because it squeaks when you chew it)—is easy to cook, but don't take your eye off it since it browns quickly and you want it golden, not burnt to a crisp.

Finely slice the fennel into a serving bowl and immediately toss it in the lemon juice to prevent oxidation.

Place a skillet over high heat, drizzle in the olive oil, and reduce the heat to medium. Add the diced halloumi and cook for about 2 minutes on each side, until golden.

Add the garlic to the fennel and mix well. Stir in the cranberries and dill. Mix well and top with the warm halloumi.

Jeweled Quinoa

serves 1

Scant ¼ cup quinoa

1 tsp bouillon powder

2 tbsp olive oil

¾ oz red onion, diced

1 garlic clove, finely chopped

Pinch of dried tarragon

½ yellow bell pepper, diced

¼ red chili, finely diced

Zest and juice of ½ lemon

Scant ¼ cup raw cashews

½ oz dried cranberries

¾ oz flat-leaf parsley, finely
chopped

1 oz feta, crumbled

(Pictured on page 91.) Cook a batch of quinoa once a week, you can then warm it up in portions. Add pomegranate seeds for a burst of color and freshness.

Measure the volume of the quinoa and bring twice the volume of water to a boil in a pan. Add the quinoa and bouillon powder, bring back to a boil, then simmer for 20 minutes, or until the "germ" separates. Drain and set aside. Meanwhile soak the dried cranberries.

Heat the oil in a large pan, add the onion and garlic, and sauté gently for 5 minutes, until softened, then add the tarragon and 2 tablespoons of water and cook for another 2-3 minutes, until the onions are soft.

Stir in the yellow bell pepper, chili, lemon juice, cashews, and drained cranberries with another 2 tablespoons of water. Add the quinoa, stir to combine, and heat through for 2-3 minutes. Remove from the heat and stir in the grated lemon zest and chopped parsley. Stir in the crumbled feta and serve warm or cold, whichever you prefer.

Raw Nutty Coleslaw

serves 2 as a side dish

2 celery stalks

1 carrot, thinly sliced
  diagonally

½ cup mixed sprouts (such
  as mung beans, alfalfa,
  sunflower)

For the dressing

1 cup raw cashews

1 tsp mustard

Juice of 1 lemon

About ½ cup water

Instead of opting for the usual artery-clogging mayonnaise version, try coating your fresh, crunchy coleslaw vegetables in this delicious, creamy, high-protein healthy alternative.

Using a potato peeler, shred the celery into long spaghetti-like strips and place in a bowl with the carrot and sprouts.

Place the cashews, mustard, and lemon juice in a blender with most of the water and blend to a smooth, creamy paste, adding more water a little at a time, if necessary.

Add the dressing to the bowl and toss gently to combine.

Caramelized Pear and Lentil Salad

serves 2

4 tbsp olive oil

1 tbsp agave syrup

1 tbsp balsamic vinegar

1 ripe pear, quartered and cored

Scant ¼ cup Puy lentils

1 vine of baby tomatoes

Scant ¼ cup walnuts, soaked for 30 minutes, drained and broken into pieces

2 scallions, thinly sliced diagonally

1 red chili, thinly sliced diagonally

Juice of ½ lemon

3½ cups arugula leaves

I love this salad as it looks beautiful and tastes unbelievably good. I like my lentils al dente and slightly nutty tasting, but if you like them more mushy then extend the cooking time a little longer.

Place 2 tablespoons of the olive oil with the agave syrup and balsamic vinegar in a shallow pan, add the pear and half-cover the pan with a lid. Simmer for 30 minutes, or until the pear is caramelized all over. Check frequently to make sure there is enough liquid, adding water a tablespoon at a time if necessary.

Meanwhile, place the Puy lentils in a pan, cover with plenty of cold water, bring to a boil, then simmer for 20–25 minutes, until al dente; cook longer if you prefer them softer. Drain and set aside.

Preheat the oven to 325°F. Place the tomatoes, still on their vine, on a baking sheet and bake for 15 minutes, or until the skins soften and start to split.

Put the walnuts, scallions, and chili in a bowl, add the lentils, the remaining olive oil, and the lemon juice, and toss gently.

To serve, arrange the arugula leaves on 2 plates, pile the lentil salad on top, and top with the pears and vine tomatoes.

NUTRITIONAL NUGGET
Puy lentils are a great source of zinc and magnesium, to support you in stressful times.

There's nothing better than a colorful salad to entice the most cynical of health phobes. I find that the more color there is, the less they complain!

Roots and Walnut Salad

**serves 1 as a main dish or
serves 2 as a side dish**

Scant ¼ cup raw walnuts,
    quartered
2 oz beet
3 oz carrot
¾ oz pear
1 scallion
1 tbsp extra virgin olive oil
1 tbsp tamari
Pinch of cayenne pepper
½ oz cilantro

(Pictured on page 96.) Beets are great for supporting the liver in its natural detoxification processes, and walnuts contain essential fats that feed the brain (it looks like two halves of the brain itself!).

An hour before you want to assemble your salad, soak the walnuts. Next, peel the beet, finely slice it, and put into a bowl. Dice the carrot and pear and finely slice the scallion. Tip into the bowl along with the soaked walnuts. Drizzle in the olive oil and tamari, sprinkle in the cayenne pepper, and mix gently.

Chop the cilantro leaves and stir in just before serving with a garnish of beautiful sprouts.

Pomegranate and Mozzarella Salad

serves 2

Seeds from 1 ruby red
    pomegranate
2 balls of mozzarella

For the dressing
2 tbsp roughly chopped flat-
    leaf parsley and mint
1 garlic clove, grated
1 red chili, deseeded and
    finely chopped
2 tbsp extra virgin olive oil
Pinch of ground cumin

(Pictured on page 97.) I find the easiest way to get pomegranate seeds out of their pods is to loosen the seeds from their pith, then allow them to drop into a big bowl of cold water; the pith floats to the surface.

Remove the seeds from the pomegranate, following my method above or using your own technique.

Drain the mozzarella balls and tear into smallish pieces (about 6–8) and arrange on 2 plates, then blend the dressing ingredients with a hand-held blender or whisk together with a fork.

To serve, drizzle the dressing over the mozzarella, then sprinkle with the pomegranate seeds.

Pulsed Fava Bean and Pearl Barley Salad

serves 1

Scant ¼ cup pearl barley
1 tsp bouillon powder
1¼ oz fava beans
2 tbsp olive oil
Juice of ½ lime
Pinch of Himalayan pink salt

1 small garlic clove
1 carrot, grated
½ oz dill, finely chopped
Pinch of ground cumin
2 broccolini stalks
½ red chili, finely sliced
  diagonally, to garnish (optional)

The combination of beans and grain here provides all eight essential amino acids for building and repairing the whole body.

Place the pearl barley and bouillon powder in a pan, add plenty of cold water, bring to a boil, then simmer for 25–30 minutes, until tender. Drain and set aside.

Place the fava beans in a blender with the olive oil, lime juice, and a pinch of salt, grate in the garlic and pulse for 1 minute to form a rough paste.

Transfer the pulsed beans to a bowl and stir in the pearl barley with the carrot, dill, and a pinch of cumin.

Meanwhile, steam the broccolini until just tender.

Serve the pulsed bean mixture with the broccolini on top, garnished with sliced red chili if you like.

Portobello Mushroom and Fennel Salad

serves 1

1 portobello mushroom
1 garlic clove, finely sliced
3 sprigs of thyme
Pinch of Himalayan pink salt
2 tbsp olive oil
3¼ oz fennel
Juice of ½ lemon
½ tbsp raw pumpkin seeds
¼ oz flat-leaf parsley, roughly
   chopped

The combination of soft-textured mushroom and crisp, cool fennel with the slight bitterness of the pumpkin seeds reaches almost every part of the palate.

Preheat the oven to 350°F.

Place the mushroom on a baking sheet and sprinkle with the garlic, thyme, and a pinch of salt, then drizzle over 1 tablespoon of the olive oil. Bake for 15 minutes, until tender.

Meanwhile, finely dice the fennel and toss with the remaining olive oil and the lemon juice.

To serve, place the mushroom on a plate, top with the fennel, and sprinkle with the pumpkin seeds and chopped parsley.

Beet, Roasted Garlic, and Quinoa Salad with Feta

serves 2

1 whole garlic bulb

1 large beet, washed and cut into eighths or 2 small beets, quartered

1 red onion, unpeeled and cut into eighths

4 tbsp olive oil

1 long vine of baby tomatoes

Generous ⅓ cup quinoa

1 tsp bouillon powder

Pinch of Himalayan pink salt

1½ oz mixed salad greens

1½ oz feta

Lemony Dressing or My Secret Salad Dressing (see page 104), to serve

The combination of textures and flavors in this dish makes my mouth water just thinking about it—contrast is the key ingredient here.

Preheat the oven to 340°F.

Chop the top off the garlic bulb so the cloves are slightly exposed and place on a baking sheet with the beet and onion. Drizzle over 2 tablespoons of the olive oil and roast for 35 minutes. Add the tomatoes, still on their vine, and cook for another 5–7 minutes, until softened.

Meanwhile, measure the volume of the quinoa and bring twice the volume of water to a boil in a pan. Add the quinoa and bouillon powder, bring back to a boil, then simmer for 20 minutes, or until the "germ" separates. Drain and set aside.

When the vegetables are cooked, hold the base of the garlic bulb in a cloth, squeeze out the soft flesh onto a chopping board, and mash it with a flat knife. Using the back of a tablespoon, very gently spread the mashed garlic over the quinoa to avoid clumping, then mix it in thoroughly. Stir in the remaining olive oil and a pinch of salt.

To serve, arrange the salad greens on 2 plates and top with the quinoa. Scatter the beet and red onion around the edge, crumble over the feta, and top with the vine tomatoes and your choice of dressing.

NUTRITIONAL NUGGET
The beta-carotene found in beets, red tomatoes, and red onion highly protects your outer and inner skin. This is a great antioxidant salad for any time of the year.

Five Salad Dressings

My Secret Salad Dressing

4 tbsp olive oil
2 tbsp tamari
2 tbsp balsamic vinegar
1 tbsp agave syrup

Simply mix together and drizzle over an eagerly awaiting salad!

Lemony Dressing

4 tbsp olive oil
2 tbsp apple cider vinegar
Juice of 1 lemon
1 small handful of cilantro
1 tbsp agave syrup

Blend with a hand-held blender or in a mini food processor until creamy.

Tangy Almond Dressing

1 heaped tbsp almond butter
3 tbsp olive oil
Finely grated zest and juice of 1 lime
1 tbsp tamari
Pinch of cayenne pepper
½-in piece of red chili, deseeded and finely chopped

Blend with a hand-held blender or in a mini food processor until smooth.

Soy Mayonnaise Dressing

1 heaped tbsp soy yogurt
1 tbsp olive oil
1 small garlic clove, grated

Stir all the ingredients together until thoroughly combined.

Clockwise from left
Choose from Tangy Almond, Lemony, My Secret Salad, Tahini and Cumin, or Soy Mayonnaise salad dressings.

People have been asking
me for years to share my
salad dressing recipes as
they can transform even
the most simple ingredients
and make them taste divine.
Enjoy!

Tahini and
Cumin Dressing

1 heaped tbsp tahini
2 tbsp olive oil
Juice of ½ lemon
1 heaped tsp ground cumin
3 tbsp water

Blend with a hand-held blender or in a mini food
processor until creamy.

mains

Mini Pizzas

makes 8

For the bases

½ tsp active dry yeast

⅔ cup lukewarm water

2¼ cups white spelt flour

½ tsp Himalayan pink salt

For the sauce

1 tbsp olive oil

1 onion, chopped

1 garlic clove

2 tbsp capers, rinsed and drained

Pinch of dried hot pepper flakes

1¾ cups tomatoes, deseeded and diced

1 tbsp fresh or 1 tsp dried oregano

(Pictured on pages 106–107.) My mother could never eat pizza because of a wheat intolerance, so it's been my mission to put pizza on her plate. And here it is! (The yield for the topping recipes opposite are per mini pizza, so double or quadruple up, as necessary.)

Preheat the oven to 400°F. Mix the yeast with the water, cover, and set aside in a warm room for about 15 minutes.

Meanwhile, make the pizza sauce by heating the oil in a pan and sautéing the onion and garlic gently until the onions start to soften, then add a splash of water to cool and add the remaining ingredients. Simmer for 15 minutes until the right consistency.

Whisk the yeast and water mixture and leave for another 5 minutes.

Place the flour and salt in a large bowl. Make a well in the center and pour in the yeast mixture. Turn out onto a work surface and knead for 5–10 minutes until smooth and silky to the touch, adding a little more flour if necessary.

Divide the bread dough into pieces, roll each piece into a ball, place on a baking sheet lined with baking parchment and flatten into a circle. Smear on some tomato sauce followed by your choice of toppings (see opposite), then bake for 5 minutes, rotate and bake for a further 5 minutes, or until ready.

NUTRITIONAL NUGGET
Spelt is an ancient wheat-based grain that is far lower in gluten than most modern wheats. The mineral content is far richer and much less processed. Many people who have a wheat intolerance are able to tolerate spelt.

Artichoke and Basil with Mozzarella

2 canned artichoke hearts, thinly
  sliced
2 basil leaves, shredded
¾ oz buffalo mozzarella, torn into
  small pieces

Zucchini and Lemon with Feta

½ oz zucchini, thinly sliced
3 strips of lemon rind, finely sliced
½ oz feta, crumbled

Fennel and Sweet Potato with Goat's Cheese

½ oz fennel, thinly sliced
½ oz sweet potato, thinly sliced
¼ oz hard goat's cheese, grated

Roasted Garlic, Beet, and Feta

3 garlic cloves, roasted and squeezed
  out of the skins
¼ oz beet, thinly sliced
½ oz feta, crumbled

When it comes to toppings for your pizzas, you can simply invent your own to suit your mood or what's in season. Here are a few of our favorites.

Spanish Omelet with Dill and Sweet Potato

serves 4

Generous 1 cup sweet potato, quartered lengthwise and thinly sliced

2 tbsp olive oil, plus extra for greasing

6 eggs

1¼ oz red bell pepper, deseeded and cut into strips

2 tbsp finely chopped dill

Pinch of Himalayan pink salt

Mixed salad greens, to serve

For variations, add

2½ oz leeks, sliced

3½ oz asparagus

This is what I always make when I'm "too tired to cook" as it's so simple to prepare and gives me so much energy. Add some thinly sliced leeks or a few asparagus spears for even more flavor and texture.

Preheat the oven to 340°F.

Arrange the sweet potato slices on a baking sheet, drizzle with the olive oil, and bake for 20 minutes, until tender. Leave the oven switched on.

Beat the eggs in a large bowl and add the sweet potato slices, red bell pepper, dill, and a pinch of salt.

Using a sheet of paper towel, coat a nonstick ovenproof skillet evenly with olive oil. Heat over a low heat, then pour in the egg mixture and cook, loosening the edge of the omelet with a spatula every 30 seconds to make sure it doesn't stick. When the eggs have set to about ¼ in from the edge of the pan, transfer the skillet to the oven and cook for 15–20 minutes. To test whether the omelet is cooked, press the top with a palette knife—no egg should ooze out.

Serve warm or cold with mixed salad greens.

NUTRITIONAL NUGGET
For vegetarians, eggs are one of the only sources of complete protein and fortunately do not, as previously thought, cause cholesterol levels to rise.

Layered Vegetable Bake

serves 4

Scant ½ cup Puy lentils

4 tbsp olive oil, plus extra for brushing

1 beefsteak tomato, roughly chopped

1 garlic clove, sliced

1 beet, diced

½ tsp tamari

1 tsp dried chives

Pinch of ground cumin

2 tbsp water

13 oz butternut squash, thinly sliced lengthwise

10 oz zucchini, thinly sliced lengthwise

This knocks the socks off any traditional lasagne I've ever tasted! Instead of the usual pasta layers I have used colorful vegetables, so it leaves you feeling much, much lighter but totally satisfied.

Preheat the oven to 340°F.

Place the lentils in a small pan, cover with water, bring to a boil, then simmer for 10–15 minutes, until al dente. Drain and set aside.

Meanwhile, heat the olive oil in a large pan and squash the tomato into the oil to make a base for the sauce. Add the garlic and beet with the tamari, chives, and a pinch of cumin. Add the water and cook over medium heat for 15 minutes, or until reduced to a thick sauce. Add the lentils to the pan with a splash more water and simmer for another 5 minutes.

Layer half the butternut squash and a third of the zucchini in an ovenproof dish and spread over half the lentil sauce. Repeat the layers, finishing with the remaining zucchini. Brush the zucchini generously with olive oil, then bake for 45 minutes, or until the vegetables are just tender.

You may also like to try using the parsley oil from the Pomegranate and Mozzarella Salad (see page 98) instead of olive oil on the top.

 WHAT IS TAMARI?
This is a wheat-free soy sauce substitute. Like soy sauce, it has a rich flavor and is dark; it's excellent in dressings and marinades.

Puy Lentil, Coconut, and Goat's Cheese Bake

serves 4

Scant ⅔ cup Puy lentils

3½ oz butternut squash, diced

3 tbsp olive oil

2 garlic cloves

Generous ¾ cup coconut milk

¾ cup firm goat's cheese, grated

1½ oz flat-leaf parsley, chopped, to garnish

½ red chili, finely sliced, to garnish

Watercress, to serve

For those who are craving a richer dish, bake away! To make lentils easier to digest, when boiling them from scratch pop a piece of kombu seaweed into the pan as this will help break down the fiber in the lentils.

Preheat the oven to 340°F.

Place the lentils in a small pan, cover with water, bring to a boil, then simmer for 10–15 minutes, until al dente. Drain and set aside.

Place the diced butternut squash on a baking sheet, drizzle with 2 tablespoons of the olive oil, and bake for 10 minutes, until nearly tender. Leave the oven switched on.

Meanwhile, heat the remaining olive oil in a pan and sauté the garlic until softened. Stir in the lentils and squash with scant ¼ cup of the coconut milk and let simmer for 5 minutes.

Pour the mixture into an ovenproof baking dish or 4 individual ramekins, pour over the remaining coconut milk, and bake for 15 minutes. Sprinkle over the grated goat's cheese and return to the oven to melt the cheese.

Serve with some watercress and sprinkled with chopped parsley and the sliced chili if you like a bit of heat.

Quinoa and Cranberry Burgers

serves 4

½ cup sweet potato, chopped

3 tbsp olive oil

½ cup quinoa

2 tsp bouillon powder

⅓ cup dried cranberries,
  soaked in water for 4 hours
  and drained

¼ oz parsley, chopped

2 heaped tbsp nutritional yeast
  flakes

1 tbsp arrowroot flour

Pinch of Himalayan pink salt

1 egg white

Olive oil, for sautéing

For the sauce

⅓ cup macadamia nuts

2 tsp tahini

1 tsp grated fresh ginger

Juice of 1 lemon

2 tbsp water

Pinch of cayenne pepper

Pinch of ground cumin

These sweet yet savory mini burgers could be your main dish, or even make them bite-size for canapés. If you don't have nutritional yeast flakes, don't worry, but they do add extra vitamin B12 and a slight cheesy taste.

To make the sauce, place all the sauce ingredients in a blender, whiz until smooth, and set aside.

Preheat the oven to 340°F.

Place the chopped sweet potato on a baking sheet, drizzle with 2 tablespoons of the olive oil, and bake for 30 minutes, until tender. Transfer to a mini food processor (or use a hand-held blender) with the remaining olive oil and blend to a purée. Increase the oven temperature to 350°F.

Meanwhile, measure the volume of the quinoa and bring twice the volume of water to a boil in a pan. Add the quinoa and bouillon powder, bring back to a boil, then simmer for 20 minutes, or until the "germ" separates. Drain and set aside.

Place the sweet potato purée in a bowl with the quinoa and the remaining ingredients and mix to a sticky consistency. Form the mixture into 8 burgers.

Heat a little olive oil in a skillet and, working in batches if necessary, cook the burgers for about 2 minutes on each side, until golden. Transfer to a baking sheet lined with baking parchment and bake for 10 minutes.

Serve the burgers at once, with the sauce.

WHAT IS HIMALAYAN PINK SALT?
This delicately pink crystalline salt originates from ancient seas. It is naturally dried by the sun and is totally pure and full of amazing minerals.

When I make a salad I look at it like
constructing a house—build up the
different layers of flavors, texture, and color
to create the "wow" factor.

Roasted Eggplant with Sumac and Tahini Dressing

serves 4

2 eggplants, cut widthwise into
    ½-in slices
Olive oil, for brushing
2 tbsp pine nuts, toasted
Large handful of basil leaves
Seeds from ½ pomegranate
    (see page 98 for how to
    remove them from the pod)
Himalayan pink salt
Freshly ground black pepper

For the dressing
Generous ⅛ cup tahini
3 tbsp extra virgin
    olive oil
3 tbsp lemon juice
4 tbsp hot water
1 garlic clove, crushed
1 tsp sumac
Himalayan pink salt

(Pictured on page 118.) This Lebanese-influenced dish tastes lighter than most eggplant dishes from that region. The sumac has a sharp lemon flavor and is a key ingredient in Middle Eastern cooking.

To make the dressing, place all the ingredients in a bowl and whisk until smooth. Taste and adjust the seasoning if necessary, then chill until required (the sauce can be stored in the fridge for up to 3 days).

Lightly brush both sides of the eggplant slices with olive oil and sprinkle with salt and black pepper.

Broil on both sides on a very hot griddle pan until soft and golden. Alternatively, roast for 20–30 minutes in a preheated oven, 425°F. (This can also be done up to 3 days in advance—store the roasted eggplant slices in the fridge, but bring to room temperature before serving.)

To serve, arrange the roasted eggplant slices on a serving dish, slightly overlapping. Drizzle with the dressing and sprinkle with toasted pine nuts, basil leaves, and pomegranate seeds.

TIP
When you add the water to the tahini and start to stir it will look like it is curdling but fret not—just keep whisking and it will become smooth.

Noodle and Smoked Tofu Salad with Mirin Dressing

serves 2

For the salad

4 oz buckwheat noodles

2 oz carrot

1¼ oz zucchini

¾ oz daikon, thinly sliced

¾ oz snow peas, thinly sliced

¾ oz mizuna leaves

¼ cup bean sprouts

2 oz pomegranate seeds, plus
   extra to garnish

4 tsp sesame oil

4 oz smoked tofu, cut into 6
   chunky squares

2 tsp tamari

Cilantro leaves

Sushi ginger

⅓ cup dry roasted cashews, to
   garnish

For the dressing

1 oz white miso paste

2 tbsp mirin

2 tsp sesame oil

2 tsp umeboshi plum purée

4 oz sushi ginger

½ tbsp rice wine vinegar

1 tbsp lime juice

Scant ⅓ cup olive oil

2 tsp water

(Pictured on page 119.) This distinctly Asian recipe is both delicious and beautiful to behold, with the carrot and zucchini spirals. The buckwheat noodles add a hearty feel to the dish.

To make the dressing, whiz all the ingredients in a blender until thick and smooth.

Use a spiralizer to make carrot and zucchini spirals. Cook the noodles according to the packet instructions, then rinse in cold water and drain well. Place in a bowl with the carrot and zucchini spirals and mix well. Mix in the remaining vegetables, pomegranate seeds, and 2 teaspoons of the sesame oil.

Just before serving, heat the remaining sesame oil in a skillet. Add the tofu and cook for 2 minutes, until brown on all sides. Add the tamari, toss to coat and glaze the tofu, and cook for 2 minutes. Thread onto 2 wooden skewers, layering the tofu cubes with whole cilantro leaves and sushi ginger.

To serve, add the dressing to the noodles and toss gently to coat. Arrange a heap of salad on each plate and scatter with roasted cashews and pomegranate seeds, then sit a tofu skewer at one side.

NUTRITIONAL NUGGET
In spite of its name, buckwheat is not related to wheat and, like quinoa, is classed as a pseudocereal. Buckwheat is particularly high in rutin, which strengthens and protects the delicate lining of our capillaries and arteries—this is a heart-healthy meal.

Sweetcorn and Fava Bean Fritters

serves 2

2 large eggs

Scant ⅔ cup frozen sweetcorn, defrosted and drained

Generous ¾ cup frozen baby fava beans, defrosted and drained

⅓ cup rice flour

2 tbsp finely chopped cilantro

1 Thai chili, deseeded and finely chopped

Juice of 1 lime

¼ tsp Himalayan pink salt

Freshly ground black pepper

Sunflower oil, for sautéing

For the dressing

2 tsp white miso

1 tsp agave syrup

1 tsp lemon juice

These colorful fritters are unbelievably delicious. They give you the impression of being substantial and really rather naughty, but leave you feeling light and bright.

To make the dressing, whisk the ingredients together and set aside.

To make the fritters, whisk the eggs in a large bowl and add the sweetcorn and fava beans. Add the flour and stir well to combine. Add the cilantro and chili with the lime juice, season with the salt and plenty of black pepper, and stir in.

Heat a little sunflower oil in a large skillet and, working in batches, cook spoonfuls of the mixture on both sides, until golden. Depending on the size you want, use 1 or 2 tablespoons of mixture for each fritter.

Serve the fritters with the Feta, Cucumber, and Spinach Salad (see opposite) and accompanied with the dressing.

NUTRITIONAL NUGGET
Sweetcorn is one of the highest sources of vitamin D—so not only do they look sunny, they are!

Feta, Cucumber, and Spinach Salad

serves 4

½ tsp bouillon powder

6 broccolini stalks

⅓ cup frozen peas, defrosted

1 small yellow bell pepper,
    deseeded and diced

1 scallion, finely sliced
    diagonally

2½ oz cucumber, diced

2-in piece of fresh ginger,
    peeled and grated

2 tbsp olive oil

Juice of 1 lemon

3½ oz feta, crumbled

2¾ oz baby spinach leaves

Place the bouillon powder in a pan with about 3 in of water, bring to a boil, add the broccolini, and simmer for 3 minutes. Add the peas and cook for another 2 minutes, until the broccolini is just tender and the peas are completely heated through. Drain and set aside.

Place the yellow bell pepper, scallion, cucumber, and ginger in a bowl, add the olive oil and lemon juice, and stir thoroughly, making sure the ginger is evenly mixed in. Add the broccolini, peas, feta, and spinach and toss gently to combine.

This can be thrown together in a nanosecond and is a perfectly balanced meal. It also makes a lovely side dish —with or without the feta, depending on the dish you are serving it with.

Spicy Tofu Skewers with a Chili Pesto Dip

serves 2

1 red onion, chopped

3 oz butternut squash, chopped

1 fennel bulb, chopped

2 tbsp olive oil, plus extra for sautéing

½ tsp harissa

7 oz tofu, cubed

Tofu loves to soak up flavors… With this easy recipe you can serve an impressively fancy dish very quickly, and the dip is just delectable!

First, make the dip (see below). Next, preheat the oven to 350°F.

Toss the chopped vegetables in 1 tablespoon of the olive oil, then place on a baking sheet and bake for 35–40 minutes.

Meanwhile, mix the harissa with the remaining olive oil in a bowl and toss the tofu cubes in the mixture. Heat a skillet, add the tofu cubes, and cook for 6 minutes, turning frequently.

Thread the tofu cubes and roasted vegetables onto wooden skewers and serve at once, with the dip and Mint-and-Mango-Marinated Zucchini Spaghetti (see page 126).

Chili Pesto Dip

2 cups arugula leaves

¼ oz dill

⅓ cup raw cashews

1¼ oz feta

Juice ½ lemon

½ tsp ground ginger

1 small red chili

1½ heaped tbsp raw sunflower seeds

1 tbsp olive oil

2 tbsp water

Place all the ingredients in a blender and whiz until beautifully smooth.

NUTRITIONAL NUGGET
The bright colors of all squashes and pumpkins pack a carotene-rich punch—generally speaking, the richer the color, the higher the concentration of carotenes, which protect against heart disease. What's more, they are an excellent source of folic acid, which is important during early pregnancy, and vitamins B1, B6, and C.

Mint-and-Mango-Marinated Zucchini Spaghetti

If you fancy some pasta while you're eating the alkaline way, then this fruity dish is definitely worth a try. This is our raw "spaghetti," and it gets everyone's head spinning at a dinner party.

serves 2

For the marinade
1 mango
4 tbsp olive oil (or more if liked)
15 mint leaves
½ tsp ground cumin
1 tsp lime juice

1-in piece of red chili
2-in piece of fresh ginger

For the spaghetti
2 zucchini, sliced lengthwise into julienne or put through a spiralizer

Peel and remove the pit from the mango. Tip the mango flesh along with all the other marinade ingredients into a blender and blend till smooth.

Pour the minty marinade over the zucchini "spaghetti" and work it in by hand. And that's it, ready to serve.

NUTRITIONAL NUGGET
Mangoes are a rich source of all sorts of phytochemicals—carotenoids, flavonoids, and antioxidants—as well as vitamin C and fiber. These plant-based chemicals protect against heart disease and stroke, and prevent certain types of cancer. Mangoes also contain enzymes that help to improve digestion. Digestive function is further enhanced by the fresh mint in this vibrant spicy marinade.

Tomato and Mushroom Dhal

serves 4

2 tbsp olive oil

1 onion, chopped

2 garlic cloves, diced

½ tsp dried parsley

¼ tsp dried cilantro

¼ tsp cumin seeds

7 oz baby vine tomatoes

2 portobello mushrooms, sliced

3⅔ cups water

2 cups split red lentils

2-in piece of red chili,
   finely diced

4 cups fresh cilantro, roughly
   chopped

2 cups fresh parsley, roughly
   chopped

2½ cups spinach (optional)

When traveling in India I was living off dhal and when I returned home I wanted to make sure I could still get my fix! This weekday staple is such a rich source of protein and is also very comforting.

Heat the olive oil in a large pan over medium heat and sauté the onion and garlic for 2 minutes or so, until they start to absorb the oil.

Stir in the dried parsley and cilantro, cumin seeds, tomatoes, and mushrooms with ⅛ cup of the water. Allow to sweat until the tomatoes start to split and the water is absorbed.

Stir in the lentils, chili, and 1⅔ cups of the remaining water and cook over medium heat for 25–30 minutes, adding the remaining water a little at a time as necessary until the lentils are cooked and reduced to a mushy consistency but still hold their shape.

To serve, stir in the fresh cilantro and parsley and the spinach, if using.

Butternut Squash Risotto

serves 4

7 oz butternut squash, diced
3 tbsp olive oil
1 red onion, chopped
2 garlic cloves, chopped
Scant 1 cup brown risotto rice
2½ cups hot vegetable stock
    made with 1 tbsp bouillon
    powder
1 handful of sage leaves,
    chopped, plus whole leaves
    to garnish
Pinch of Himalayan pink salt

Remember to stir stir stir this risotto, as that is what will make it super-creamy and rich. The stirring of the dish is almost therapeutic and meditative after a busy day, and it's well worth the time and effort.

Preheat the oven to 350°F.

Place the diced butternut squash on a baking sheet, drizzle with 2 tablespoons of the olive oil, and bake for 15 minutes, until nearly tender.

Heat the remaining olive oil in a wide-bottomed pan over medium heat, add the onion and garlic and cook for 2–3 minutes, until softened. Add the rice and cook, stirring constantly, for 1 minute to coat the rice in oil, then reduce the heat and stir in 2 large ladlefuls of stock. Simmer, stirring gently, over low heat until the rice has absorbed the stock, then continue adding the stock a ladleful at a time and stirring gently until it is absorbed before adding another ladleful.

After 30 minutes stir in the butternut squash and the chopped sage leaves, then continue to add the stock until the rice is cooked but al dente—this will take about 50 minutes. Season with a pinch of salt.

Serve at once, garnished with whole sage leaves.

TIP
Once you have become familiar with how to make this dish, try replacing the butternut squash with other vegetables for a different flavor or texture. Remember that the harder the vegetable, the longer you need to cook it, and vice versa for softer veg—if you are using mushrooms, for instance, you only need to throw them in at the end.

Red Rice and Beet Risotto

serves 4

2 tbsp olive oil
1 red onion, chopped
2 garlic cloves, chopped
Scant 1 cup Camargue red rice
2½ cups hot vegetable stock,
   made with 1 tbsp bouillon
   powder
Generous 1 cup beet, cubed
1 handful of parsley, chopped
3½ oz feta

This might take a little more time than a normal risotto but my oh my, doesn't it taste delicious? The vibrancy of the red rice along with the juice from the beet makes this dish look so beautiful.

Heat the olive oil in a wide-bottomed pan over medium heat, add the onion and garlic, and cook for 2–3 minutes, until softened.

Add the rice and cook, stirring constantly, for 1 minute to coat the rice in oil, then reduce the heat and stir in 2 large ladlefuls of stock. Simmer, stirring gently, over low heat until the rice has absorbed the stock, then continue adding the stock a ladleful at a time and stirring gently until it is absorbed before adding another ladleful.

After 10 minutes of cooking, add the beet chunks. After 25 minutes, add most of the chopped parsley, then continue to add the stock until the rice is cooked but al dente—this will take 30–40 minutes. At the last minute, stir in most of the feta to make the risotto wonderfully creamy.

Serve garnished with the remaining feta and chopped parsley.

Pea Carbonara

serves 2

3 tbsp olive oil

1 shallot, diced

2 small garlic cloves,
thinly sliced

Scant 2 cups frozen peas,
defrosted and drained

⅔ cup fava beans (fresh,
shelled, or frozen, defrosted
and drained)

Himalayan pink salt

Freshly ground black pepper

6 oz gluten-free spaghetti

2 egg yolks

¾ cup hard goat's cheese,
grated

Leaves from 2 large handfuls of
fresh mint, half chopped and
half left whole

1 red chili, sliced diagonally, to
garnish (optional)

Who says you can't indulge in a yummy bowl of creamy pasta? I was not prepared to give up this wonderful dish from my childhood—so we found a way to make it the Honestly Healthy way!

Heat the olive oil in a pan and sauté the shallots, garlic, peas, and fava beans over medium heat, partially covered, until the shallots are soft. Season to taste with salt and pepper.

Meanwhile, bring a large pan of salted water to a boil and add the spaghetti. Cook according to the packet instructions, then drain well.

In a bowl, mix the egg yolks with half the goat's cheese and the chopped mint and season with black pepper.

Using tongs, transfer the cooked, drained spaghetti to the pan with the shallot mixture. Pour in the egg mixture, turning the spaghetti into the mixture with the tongs over a very low heat to coat the pasta and thicken the egg mixture.

Serve sprinkled with the remaining grated cheese and garnished with chili slices, if you like, and whole mint leaves.

TIP
Wheat-free pasta tends to disintegrate quite easily so be gentle when coating it with the sauce.

Spicy Bean Burgers with Cajun Wedges and Superslaw

serves 4

1½ tbsp olive oil

1 tsp ground coriander

1 tsp turmeric

2 fat garlic cloves, chopped

1 small red chili, chopped

½ cup onion, chopped

2½ oz carrot, grated

2½ oz zucchini, grated

Scant ⅓ cup fresh or frozen
   sweetcorn kernels

1¼ cups canned black-eyed
   beans, rinsed and drained

1¼ cups canned black beans,
   rinsed and drained

1 tsp Himalayan pink salt

1 tbsp chopped fresh cilantro

¼ cup millet flakes

Cornmeal, for coating

Sunflower oil, for sautéing

To serve

Cajun Sweet Potato Wedges
   (see page 136)

Superslaw (see page 136)

There's nothing better than sinking your teeth into a (healthy) burger and indulging in some homemade spicy potato wedges and slaw, to boot.

Heat the oil in a large saucepan, add the ground coriander and turmeric and sauté for 2 minutes, then add the garlic and chili and sauté for 1–2 minutes, until softened. Add the onion and sauté for another 3–4 minutes to soften the onion, adding a splash of water if the mixture gets too dry.

Add the grated carrot and zucchini and sauté for 1–2 minutes, until softened. Add the sweetcorn kernels and sauté for 2 minutes, until softened. Add the beans and sauté for another 2 minutes, until softened. Stir in the salt.

Transfer the ingredients to a mixing bowl and stir in the chopped cilantro and millet flakes. When cool enough to handle, form the mixture into 8 burgers, kneading the mixture lightly to break down the beans.

Spread a generous layer of cornmeal on a plate and coat the burgers well, then chill in the refrigerator for 30 minutes.

Meanwhile, preheat the oven to 325°F.

Heat a little sunflower oil in a skillet and, working in batches, cook the burgers for about 2 minutes on each side, until golden. Transfer to a baking sheet lined with baking parchment and bake for 20 minutes, until cooked through.

Serve hot alongside Cajun Sweet Potato Wedges and Superslaw.

Cajun Sweet Potato Wedges

serves 4

3 sweet potatoes, peeled and
   cut into large wedges
2 tbsp olive oil
Cajun spice mix, to taste

Place the sweet potato wedges in a large bowl with the olive oil and Cajun spice mix, to taste, and toss well to coat thoroughly. Transfer to a baking sheet and cook in a preheated oven, 325°F, for 30 minutes, or until golden brown.

No need to feel guilty with these—they are far healthier than fries from a diner.

Superslaw

serves 4

¼ cup red cabbage, finely sliced
Scant ½ cup white cabbage,
   finely sliced
2 oz sweet potato, grated
2 oz celeriac, grated
2 oz apple, grated
1 oz scallion, finely sliced
Generous ⅛ cup raw sunflower
   seeds, soaked for 30 minutes
   and drained
1 tsp Himalayan pink salt
Ground black pepper

Tahini/cashew mayo
1 heaped tbsp tahini
1 heaped tsp cashew butter
1 tbsp olive oil
Juice of ½ lime
½ tsp white miso
2 garlic cloves
Himalayan pink salt
Freshly ground pepper

To make the tahini/cashew mayo, whiz all the ingredients in a blender, gradually adding as much water as necessary to make a smooth sauce. Season with salt and pepper, to taste.

Combine the coleslaw ingredients in a large bowl. Pour over the mayo and, using your hands, massage together until all the coleslaw ingredients are well coated with the mayo.

Why not make up a big batch of the "mayo"— you can store it in the fridge for up to five days and use it as a creamy salad dressing.

WHAT IS WHITE MISO?
Great for light dishes, white miso is fermented for only 2–8 weeks, unlike all other misos. It has a creamy texture and is fantastic for salad dressings.

Sweet and Sour Tofu

serves 4

3½ oz carrots
1 tbsp soybean paste
Scant 1¼ cups boiling water
3½ oz fresh ginger, thinly sliced
1 lemongrass stalk, peeled and
    finely chopped
10 plum tomatoes, diced
½ green bell pepper, diced
½ red bell pepper, diced
⅓ cup edamame beans
½ onion, thinly sliced
1 tsp tamari
1 tbsp honey
½ cup smoked tofu, cubed
Cooked brown rice, to serve
Toasted cashews, to garnish

I have always wanted to find an alternative to this classic Chinese dish as I do enjoy the taste, but obviously wanted something that was healthier—and I am so glad I have.

Thinly slice the carrots on the diagonal and blanch in a pan of boiling water for 1 minute.

In a separate pan, dissolve the soybean paste in the measured amount of boiling water, then add the ginger and lemongrass. Bring the mixture to a boil, then simmer for 25–30 minutes, until reduced and infused with flavor.

Add the diced tomatoes and cook for about 5 minutes, until reduced. Add the peppers, edamame beans, and onion and cook for 3 minutes. Stir in the tamari and honey, then add the tofu and heat through.

Serve with rice, garnished with toasted cashews.

Chickpea and Sweet Potato Stew

serves 4

2 tbsp olive oil

1 red onion, finely sliced

2 garlic cloves, finely sliced

2½ cups water

1 sweet potato, cut into 1-in cubes

5 large vine tomatoes, cut into quarters

3 fresh or dried bay leaves

½ red chili, finely chopped

1 tsp ground cumin

Pinch of cayenne pepper

1 small eggplant, quartered lengthwise and cut into ½-in slices

4 cups canned chickpeas, rinsed and drained

Cilantro, roughly chopped, to serve

Cooked brown rice, to serve (optional)

I leave the skin on the sweet potato as it contains so many nutrients and is very tasty—just make sure you scrub well before cooking. Vine tomatoes are delicious but you can use plum or beefsteak tomatoes instead. This is a perfect cozy lunch or dinner on a cold day.

Heat the olive oil in a large pan over medium heat, stir in the onion and garlic, and cook for 3–4 minutes, until softened. Add scant ¼ cup of the water and stir in the sweet potato, then crush the chopped tomatoes into the pan and add the bay leaves. Cook for 5 minutes.

Add the chili, cumin, cayenne, and scant 1¼ cups of the water and simmer for 15 minutes, or until reduced to a thick sauce. Add the eggplant, chickpeas, and remaining water and simmer for another 10 minutes, stirring frequently, until the eggplant is tender and the sauce is reduced.

Serve the stew, sprinkled with some chopped cilantro, on its own or with brown rice.

NUTRITIONAL NUGGET
Did you know that cayenne pepper helps you to lose weight because of its thermogenic properties, which raise metabolism?

No one can resist a curry and movie night, least of all me! So simple to pull together and a great one to prepare the day before as the flavors just get more intense.

Thai Yellow Curry with Jasmine Brown Rice

serves 2

For the curry paste

3 shallots, chopped

1 lemongrass stalk, peeled and chopped

2 small red chilies, deseeded

5 garlic cloves

½ handful of cilantro

2-in piece of galangal, peeled and chopped

1 fresh or dried kaffir lime leaf

1 tbsp ground coriander seeds

1½ tbsp mild chili powder

½ tsp turmeric

2 tsp rice syrup

¼ tsp Himalayan pink salt

For the curry

1 lemongrass stalk

1 tbsp coconut oil

5 heaped tsp curry paste

3 oz eggplant

1⅔ cups coconut milk

2½ oz yellow bell pepper

1¾ oz sugar snap peas

2 oz fine asparagus

2½ oz red and yellow cherry tomatoes, halved

⅔ cup water

4 Thai basil leaves, shredded

Tamari, to taste

(Pictured on page 140.) If you have never made a curry paste from scratch, this is the easiest one to start with. It's worth the effort and makes you feel like a culinary genius! Serve with jasmine brown rice for authenticity.

To make the paste, whiz all the ingredients in a blender until smooth.

Next, make the curry. Peel and pound the lemongrass to release the flavor, and chop into pieces. Heat the coconut oil and sauté the lemongrass over low heat for 2 minutes to infuse the oil. Add the curry paste and sauté for 2 minutes.

Halve the eggplant lengthwise and thinly slice and simmer in generous ¾ cup of the coconut milk for 5 minutes. Cut the bell pepper into strips and pop that in the pan and simmer for another 5 minutes.

Add the sugar snap peas, asparagus, and tomatoes, the remaining coconut milk, and as much water as required to make the consistency you like and cook for 4–5 minutes, until the vegetables are just tender. Stir in the basil and a splash of tamari, to taste.

I like this curry served with some jasmine brown rice sprinkled with toasted sesame seeds and grated lime zest.

TIP
Take care not to overheat the oil and burn the spices, as this will distort the wondrous flavor of the curry.

Mung Bean Curry

serves 4

½ tsp coconut oil

1 red onion, chopped

1 tsp finely chopped garlic
   cloves

1 tsp grated fresh ginger

3–4 small red or green chilies,
   finely chopped

1 heaped tsp soybean paste

1 tsp ground cinnamon

1½ tsp turmeric

1 tsp paprika

2 fresh or dried kaffir lime
   leaves

3 plum tomatoes, chopped

1 sweet potato, diced

1²/₃ cups coconut milk

Generous ²/₃ cup split mung
   beans, soaked for 1 hour and
   cooked

1 handful of baby spinach
   leaves (optional)

Cilantro, chopped, to garnish

Brown rice, to serve

(Pictured on page 141.) No need for an introduction to this one. Everyone loves this dish, even children, as it's so warming and comforting but leaves you feeling light.

Heat the coconut oil in a large pan, then wipe the pan with a piece of paper towel so that it is lightly coated. Add the onion, garlic, ginger, chilies, and soybean paste and sauté for 2–3 minutes to soften the onion.

Add the spices, lime leaves, and tomatoes and cook for another 2–3 minutes to soften the tomatoes. Add the sweet potato and cook for 3 minutes, then add the coconut milk and mung beans. Simmer for 15–20 minutes, until the sweet potato is tender.

Adding a handful of spinach at the end is a nice touch or just add chopped cilantro as a garnish. Serve with brown rice.

NUTRITIONAL NUGGET
The mung bean has one of the widest ranges of nutrients of any bean or legume and is as versatile in its uses. This is a real energy food.

Raw Pad Thai

serves 2

2 zucchini

1 carrot

¾ oz edamame beans

2 oz snow peas, thinly sliced
  diagonally

2 oz fine asparagus, thinly
  sliced diagonally

For the sauce

Scant ⅓ cup raw cashews,
  soaked for 2 hours

3 fresh or dried dates

1 lemongrass stalk, peeled
  and chopped

½ oz fresh ginger, chopped

2 fat garlic cloves

Grated zest and juice of 1 lime

1 tbsp tamari

1 tsp dried hot pepper flakes

To garnish

1 tbsp finely chopped cilantro

Lightly toasted cashews

1 scallion, thinly sliced
  diagonally

This is such a fun one to prepare, especially if you have kids, as the spiralizer is a great implement to play with. Of course, the grown-ups enjoy it too.

To make the sauce, drain the cashews and then whiz all the ingredients in a blender, gradually adding water until smooth.

Spiralize the zucchini and carrot to make thin noodles and place in a bowl. Add the edamame beans, snow peas, and asparagus. Pour over the sauce and mix to coat the vegetables evenly.

Serve garnished with chopped cilantro, cashews, and scallion.

Eggplant with Cashew Pesto

serves 2

1 eggplant, halved lengthwise
4 tbsp olive oil
⅓ cup raw cashews
2½ cups cilantro
1 garlic clove
¼ cup feta, crumbled

This simple but tasty bake takes no effort whatsoever and (although meatless) is a meaty and complete meal, with the cashews adding great protein to this dish.

Preheat the oven to 340°F.

Place the eggplant halves cut-side up on a baking sheet, drizzle with 2 tablespoons of the olive oil, and bake for about 25 minutes, until almost tender.

Meanwhile, whiz the cashews, cilantro, garlic, and remaining olive oil in a blender to a rough paste. When the eggplant halves are almost tender, coat them with the pesto and return to the oven for another 10 minutes, until the pesto starts to crisp and brown.

Serve sprinkled with feta and accompanied with Sweet Tomato Tabbouleh (see below).

Sweet Tomato Tabbouleh

serves 2

½ cup baby vine tomatoes, deseeded, diced, and drained
4 cups flat-leaf parsley, roughly chopped
Scant ¼ cup raw sesame seeds
2 tbsp olive oil
Juice of 2 lemons
2 tsp agave syrup

Place the diced tomatoes in a bowl and stir in the parsley and sesame seeds. Whisk together the remaining ingredients and drizzle onto the tomato mixture and toss together.

NUTRITIONAL NUGGET
Parsley is very high in iron to keep you going all day.

This refreshing, zingy salad is honestly one of my favorites —I could sit and eat a whole bowlful without getting bored! The sesame seeds are a rich source of minerals, including calcium and selenium.

treats and snacks

Granola Bars

makes 12

Scant 2¼ cups jumbo rolled oats

Generous 1⅛ cups dried dates, chopped

⅔ cup dried figs, chopped

Scant ⅔ cup goji berries

Scant ½ cup dried blueberries

Scant ½ cup raisins

2 tbsp raw flax seeds

Pinch of ground cinnamon

½ tsp vanilla extract

½ tbsp lúcuma powder

1 tbsp maca powder

2 tbsp raw pumpkin seeds

1 tbsp agave syrup

NUTRITIONAL NUGGET
Nothing beats your own granola bars for ensuring additive-free, B-vitamin-rich, high-energy snack bars.

(Pictured on pages 148–149.) These perfect guilt-free snacks are full of nutrient-dense superfoods (goji berries, lúcuma and maca powder, blueberries and agave syrup), which are rich in antioxidants and so help to heal and feed your body, giving you more energy and great health. Everyone loves these and can't quite believe that they taste so great and are so good for you. Let them cool completely before demolishing!

Preheat the oven to 300°F.

Spread the oats on a large baking sheet and bake for about 20 minutes, or until golden brown, turning them over every 5 minutes or so. Remove from the oven and let cool on the baking sheet.

Place the dates and figs in a pan and cover with water to double the depth. Bring to a boil, then simmer for about 45 minutes, stirring occasionally and adding extra water if the mixture gets too dry. This is going to be your syrup, so you want to reduce the dates and figs to a sloppy, sweet liquid. The cooking time will depend on how dry the fruit is—the drier it is, the longer it will take. Once the mixture has turned into a syrup, take the pan off the heat.

Add the goji berries, blueberries, raisins, and flax seeds, and let the mixture rest for 10 minutes to let the berries and raisins swell and absorb some of the syrup.

Stir in the cinnamon, vanilla extract, lúcuma, maca, pumpkin seeds, and agave syrup. Add the oats, a little at a time, stirring after each addition to make sure they are completely coated in the syrup.

Spread the sweet oaty mixture evenly in a large rectangular baking sheet, to a thickness of about ¾ in. Bake for 15–20 minutes, until lovely and golden.

Remove the granola from the oven and cut it into 12 squares. As soon as they are cool enough to handle, carefully transfer them to a wire rack, placing them upside down, and let cool completely.

Chocolate Peanut Butter Cups

makes 6

½ cup raw cacao butter
4 tbsp agave syrup
¾ cup raw cacao powder
1 cup unsalted peanuts
2 tbsp coconut oil
1 tsp nutritional yeast flakes

I grew up on Reese's peanut butter cups, so recreating this far healthier option was like taking a trip down memory lane for my taste buds!

Place the cacao butter and agave syrup in a Vitamix or high-speed blender and blend on high speed until liquid, then add the cacao powder and blend again to combine. Transfer to a bowl, then coat the bottom and sides of 6 mini paper muffin liners with the chocolate, reserving enough to make a lid for each one. Place in the freezer for 4 minutes to set.

Meanwhile, wash and dry the blender jug and whiz the remaining ingredients to form a smooth butter. Divide the peanut butter between the chocolate cups and pour a layer of chocolate over the top. Return to the freezer for 5–10 minutes to set. Store in an airtight container in the refrigerator.

Sticky Seed Granola Bars

makes 10–12

1 cup chopped pitted dates

Scant 2 cups water

1 cup raw cashews

1 cup raw hazelnuts

3⅓ cups jumbo rolled oats

Scant 1 cup raw pumpkin seeds

Scant 1 cup raw sunflower seeds

Scant 1⅓ cups agave syrup or runny honey

½ cup mixed raw pumpkin, sunflower, and sesame seeds, for the topping

The joy of these granola bars is that, being homemade, there are no added nasties to ruin a good intention, such as the refined sugar used as a preservative in commercial versions. Using a range of nuts and seeds packs in the protein and provides masses of beneficial fats that feed the brain and skin and lift your mood. You'll love these.

Preheat the oven to 325°F.

Place the dates and scant 1 cup of the water in a pan, bring to a boil, then simmer until the dates are soft. Transfer to a blender, whiz to a paste, and pour into a large mixing bowl.

Place the cashews and hazelnuts in the blender with the remaining water and whiz to a smooth cream. Add to the bowl with the dates.

Place the oats, pumpkin seeds, and sunflower seeds in a food processor and pulse for about 1 minute, or until roughly chopped. Add these to the mixture in the bowl. Stir in the agave syrup or honey and mix thoroughly.

Transfer the mixture to a baking sheet lined with baking parchment and spread out to a thickness of ½–¾ in. Sprinkle with the mixed seeds and bake for 20 minutes, until golden.

Let cool in the baking sheet, then cut into slices.

WHAT IS AGAVE SYRUP?
Sometimes described as agave nectar, this sugar alternative is naturally extracted from the inner core of the cactus-like agave plant. Unlike refined sugar, agave syrup is absorbed slowly into the bloodstream, thereby avoiding the sugar highs and lows associated with refined sugar.

I love the fact that I can have a sweet treat, safe in the knowledge that it's also good for me!

Chocolate Coconut Balls

makes 12

10 fresh dates, pitted
½ cup raw cacao powder
generous ⅛ cup raw almonds
4 cups coconut flakes
1½ tbsp agave syrup
2 tbsp coconut oil
1 tsp xylitol
2 tbsp water

(Pictured on page 154.) Who can resist a super-cute and tasty chocolate ball? Not me! If you need your chocolate fix, then this one will hit the spot.

Preheat the oven to 350°F.

Mix the dates, cacao powder, and almonds in a blender or food processor for about 1 minute to make a sticky, chunky paste. Add the remaining ingredients and blend to a rough consistency.

Transfer the mixture to a bowl, divide it into 12 pieces, and roll into balls. Place them on a baking sheet lined with baking parchment and bake for 10 minutes, then allow to cool.

Raw Mango Coconut Balls

makes 20

3½ cups dry unsweetened
    shredded coconut
1½ cups dried unsweetened
    unsulfured mango, soaked
    in water for 30 minutes and
    drained
2 tbsp agave syrup
8 tbsp coconut oil
2 tsp freshly grated lemon zest

(Pictured on page 155.) For a mid-morning pick-me-up try these powerful little balls of natural sweetness—they will literally melt in your mouth.

Place 3¼ cups of the coconut in a food processor with the mango, agave syrup, coconut oil, and lemon zest and pulse until the mixture comes together. Transfer this to a bowl.

Put the remaining coconut in a separate bowl. Form the mixture into small balls and coat them in the coconut.

Freeze the coconut balls for 20 minutes on a baking sheet lined with baking parchment. Store in an airtight container in the refrigerator.

Nutty Cookies

makes 15

¾ cup raw Brazil nuts

1½ cups raw almonds

Scant 1⅔ cups coconut flakes

1 cup dried prunes

½ cup dried apricots

Generous ⅛ cup raw sunflower
    seeds

Generous ¼ cup raw pumpkin
    seeds

Finely grated zest of 1 lemon

About 2 tbsp apple juice

These are surely contenders for the winners of "the healthiest cookies in the world" competition, but that doesn't mean they can't pack in great flavor.

Preheat the oven to 300°F.

Place the ingredients in a food processor and whiz until the mixture comes together, adding a little extra apple juice if necessary.

Divide the mixture into 15 pieces and shape into balls. Place on a baking sheet lined with baking parchment and flatten each ball to a thickness of ¼ in.

Bake for 15 minutes, or until just firm, and then cool on a wire rack.

"Cheesy" Kale Chips

The first time I tried a kale chip I was simply blown away at its sheer super-tastiness. I couldn't quite believe that a dehydrated vegetable could be both quite so delicious and quite so nutritious.

makes 2½ oz

¼ oz thyme leaves
Juice of 1 lemon
2½ oz nutritional yeast flakes
⅔ cup raw cashews
½ cup water
2½ oz kale, chopped into 2-in pieces

Whiz all the ingredients, except the kale, in a blender until smooth. Pour the mixture over the kale pieces and, using your hands, coat the kale pieces gently but thoroughly.

Spread out on a dehydrator sheet and place in the dehydrator for 10 hours. (If you don't have a dehydrator, turn to page 54 for how to get the effect using an oven.)

NUTRITIONAL NUGGET
Sources of B12 are limited for vegetarians and vegans so these tasty little flakes of nutritional yeast are a great way of getting this exuberant vitamin into your life.

Coconut Bread

makes 1 small loaf

2¼ cups wholegrain spelt flour

2 tsp baking powder

2 tsp ground cinnamon

Scant 2⅔ cups dry
   unsweetened shredded
   coconut

Scant ⅓ cup goat's butter, plus
   extra for greasing

Scant ½ cup agave syrup

2 eggs

Scant 1¼ cups Brown Rice Milk
   (see page 57)

1 tsp vanilla extract

Yes, you can have your cake and eat it! This wondrous coconut bread will satisfy anyone's sweet tooth and makes a perfect afternoon treat.

Preheat the oven to 350°F. Grease a small loaf pan (7½ x 3½ in) with goat's butter.

Sift the flour, baking powder, cinnamon, and ground coconut flakes into a bowl.

In a separate bowl, cream the goat's butter with the agave syrup. Add the eggs, milk, and vanilla and then stir well to combine. Add the wet ingredients to the dry ingredients and combine.

Transfer the mixture to the loaf pan and bake for about 1 hour. The loaf will rise slightly and have a golden crust. To test whether it is cooked, insert the tip of a sharp knife or a skewer into the center of the loaf. If it comes out clean, the loaf is ready.

Let cool in the pan for 10 minutes, then turn out onto a wire rack to cool completely.

Nut Butter

To make any nut butter, simply blend however many nuts you need for your portion until creamy; the nut oils make it beautifully buttery.

Our favorites: almond butter and cashew butter.

TIP
When you are making your nut butter, if your blender is struggling to cream the nuts just add a few drops of olive oil.

Spelt Soda Bread

makes 1 large loaf

4 cups wholegrain spelt flour

1 tsp Himalayan pink salt

1 tsp baking soda

1 oz goat's butter

Scant ⅔ cup raw walnuts, chopped

1 egg

Scant 1¼ cups sheep's yogurt

2–3 tbsp water

This is a great alternative for people on a yeast-free plan because the baking soda acts in the same way as yeast, delivering a dense yet light, delicious bread.

Preheat the oven to 425°F.

Sift the flour, salt, and baking soda into a large bowl. Blend in the butter until the mixture resembles fine breadcrumbs, then stir in the walnuts. Whisk the egg into the yogurt and stir into the flour mixture, adding water as necessary to make a soft dough.

Form into a round and place on a greased baking sheet. Bake for 10 minutes, then reduce the heat to 375°F and cook for another 30–40 minutes, until well risen and the loaf sounds hollow when tapped underneath. Cool on a wire rack.

Sweet Potato Bread

makes 1 small loaf

½ oz fresh yeast

Scant ⅔ cup warm water

Scant 1 cup wholegrain spelt flour

Generous ¾ cup rye flour

9¼ oz sweet potato, grated, squeezed to release excess juice, and patted dry

Sunflower oil, for greasing

You will find sweet potato snuck into a few of our baking recipes as it's such a great healthy "cheat" to make anything sweet and moist.

Mix the fresh yeast with half the water, cover, and set aside in a warm room for about 15 minutes, or until the mixture starts to froth.

Mix the flours and sweet potato in a large bowl, make a well in the center and add the yeast liquid and remaining water. Mix thoroughly. Turn the dough out onto a lightly floured surface and knead for 10 minutes. Return to the bowl, cover, and proof for 30 minutes in a warm room until almost doubled in size.

Punch down the dough and form into a round loaf. Pop on a greased baking sheet, cover, and proof for another 30 minutes. Meanwhile, preheat the oven to 340°F. Bake the loaf for 40 minutes until well risen. Cool on a wire rack.

Spelt Bread

makes 1 x 1 lb loaf

1¾ cups spelt, rye, barley, or
   kamut flour
1 tbsp baking powder
¼ tsp Himalayan pink salt
1 tbsp olive oil
scant 1 cup water
1 tbsp date syrup or molasses

If you've given wheat the heave-ho then give this great wheat-free bread a whirl. The mineral content in all these grains is simply superb.

Preheat the oven to 375°F.

Mix the dry ingredients in a large bowl. Then, stir the olive oil into the water and stir into the flour. The mixture should be like a thick batter. Transfer to a small loaf pan (7½ x 3½ in) and bake for 50–55 minutes, until well risen.

Halfway through baking, brush the top with the molasses or date syrup to give color to the crust. Turn out onto a wire rack to cool.

Seeded Spelt Bread

makes 1 small loaf

½ oz fresh yeast
Scant ⅔ cup warm water
Scant 1 cup wholegrain spelt
   flour
Generous ¾ cup rye flour
½ tsp toasted fennel seeds
½ tsp black onion seeds
½ tsp mustard seeds
Sunflower oil, for greasing

This gorgeously flavorsome bread has the spices hiding in the dough, so is a great accompaniment to any savory dish.

Mix the fresh yeast with half the water, cover, and set aside in a warm room for about 15 minutes, or until the mixture starts to froth.

Mix together the flours and seeds in a large bowl. Make a well in the center and add the yeast liquid and the remaining water. Mix thoroughly. Turn the dough out onto a lightly floured surface and knead for 10 minutes. Return to the bowl, cover, and proof for 30 minutes until the dough has almost doubled in size.

Punch down the dough and form into a round loaf or break into rolls. Place on a greased baking sheet, cover, and proof for 30 minutes more. Meanwhile, preheat the oven to 340°F. Bake the loaf for 40 minutes, until well risen and the loaf sounds hollow when tapped underneath (rolls will need slightly less time, 25–30 minutes). Cool on a wire rack.

This bright and beautiful page shows you how vibrant your table can look—so say goodbye to all those cynics who think vegetarian food both looks and tastes like cardboard!

Beet and Walnut Dip

serves 3–4

Scant 1 cup cooked beet,
   roughly chopped
1–2 garlic cloves, crushed
1 small bunch of cilantro,
   roughly chopped
1 small bunch of parsley,
   roughly chopped
½ cup walnuts
3 tsp extra virgin olive oil
2 tsp red wine vinegar
Himalayan pink salt
Freshly ground black pepper

(Pictured on page 164.) The combination of sweet and bitter flavors really whets the palate. Try it as a great afternoon snack or eaten as an appetizer.

Place the beet, garlic, cilantro, parsley, and walnuts in a food processor and whiz to a coarse paste. Transfer the mixture to a bowl, add the olive oil and red wine vinegar, season with salt and pepper, and stir to combine.

Serve with crudités or as part of a salad.

Smoky Eggplant Dip

serves 3–4

2 large eggplant
1½ tbsp tahini
2 garlic cloves
Juice of 1 lemon
Olive oil, to garnish
Sumac, to garnish
Bread or crudités, to serve

To create this dip's wonderful smoky taste, cook the eggplant over a naked flame, over a medium heat on the stove, on an outside grill or barbecue, or in a very hot oven. The smell of the skin burning is exactly what you want.

Cook the eggplant for about 5 minutes, until very soft, turning frequently. When the eggplant are cool enough to handle, rip off the stalks and peel away the skin.

Whiz the eggplant flesh in a blender with the tahini, garlic, and lemon juice until smooth.

Serve in a bowl garnished with a swirl of olive oil and a sprinkle of sumac accompanied with wheat-free bread or crudités.

NUTRITIONAL NUGGET
Garlic supports liver function, and tahini is a rich source of the antioxidant selenium, as well as being a vegetarian protein.

Raw Flax Seed Crackers

makes 10 crackers

6½ oz carrots, roughly chopped

Scant 1½ cups tomatoes,
 roughly chopped

Scant 1¼ cups cilantro

⅓ cup water

½ oz scallion, finely chopped

Juice of ½ lemon

Pinch of Himalayan pink salt

Pinch of ground cumin

Generous ⅛ cup raw flax seeds,
 soaked for 2 hours

(Pictured on page 165.) Imagine sitting in Italy and smelling the aromas of all the local foods—well, this über-healthy cracker tastes like a Mediterranean scene and just fills your taste buds with love!

Blend the carrots, tomatoes, and cilantro with the water to a rough pulp, then transfer to a strainer and drain well. Place in a mixing bowl and add the flax, scallion, lemon juice, and a pinch each of salt and cumin. Drain the seeds, squeezing out as much liquid as possible with the back of a wooden spoon. Add them to the rest of the ingredients and stir well to combine.

Spread the mixture out on a dehydrator sheet to a thickness of ¾ in—it will shrink! Place in the dehydrator and dehydrate for 10 hours (see also page 54). Break into crackers when dried.

Spinach and Chickpea Hummus

serves 4

2 cups canned chickpeas,
 rinsed and drained

2¼ cups spinach

1 tbsp tahini

Juice of ½ lemon

2 tbsp olive oil

1 small garlic clove

About ½ cup water

(Pictured on page 165.) Chickpeas are the perfect base for any flavor or seasoning. I love the color the spinach adds to this yummy dip.

Place the chickpeas, spinach, tahini, lemon juice, and olive oil in a blender, grate in the garlic clove and whiz to a paste, gradually adding the water until it forms the consistency you like.

desserts

Blueberry Polenta Cake

serves 10

2 cups blueberries

4 large eggs

7 oz xylitol

1½ tsp vanilla extract

Seeds from ¼ vanilla bean

1 cup sunflower oil, plus extra
   for greasing

1 cup apple juice

2 cups white spelt flour

Scant ⅔ cup fine cornmeal

1 tsp baking powder

(Pictured on pages 168–169). This is a show-stopper of a cake! The color of the blueberries when they have burst on the surface is irresistible. Serve with some raw vanilla ice cream and you have a perfect indulgence.

Preheat the oven to 350°F. Place the blueberries in the bottom of a greased 9-in springform cake pan, base-lined with baking parchment.

Beat the eggs with the xylitol and the vanilla extract and seeds until foamy. Beat in the oil, then the apple juice. Sift in the flour, cornmeal, and baking powder, then fold in, making sure there are no lumps. Pour the batter into the cake pan and bake for 1½ hours, or until a skewer inserted into the cake comes out clean.

Let cool in the pan, then release the side of the pan, place a serving plate over the cake, and quickly flip it over so the blueberries are now on the top. Very carefully remove the baking parchment.

Raw Chocolate Mousse

serves 2

1 tbsp coconut oil

1 avocado

1 tsp water

2 heaped tbsp raw cacao
   powder

2 tbsp agave syrup (or more, to
   taste)

Raspberries or blackberries,
   to serve

Try this fun party game—ask your guests what unexpected green ingredient they think is in this velvety mousse. They will never guess!

Melt the coconut oil in a heatproof bowl set over a pan of hot water, then transfer to a blender with the avocado flesh and water and whiz until very smooth. Add the cacao powder and agave syrup or honey and whiz again until completely smooth. Taste and add a little more agave syrup, if required.

Put the mousse in a dish for two or, if you prefer, divide the mixture between 2 ramekins. Chill in the refrigerator for at least 1 hour.

Serve with raspberries or blackberries... delicious!

Not so naughty and oh soooo nice!

Sweet-Potato Chocolate Brownies

makes 8

Generous ¾ cup rice flour

¾ cup raw cacao powder

¼ tsp baking powder

6 oz sweet potato, cooked and
  mashed to a purée

Scant ¾ cup date syrup

Scant ¾ cup goat's butter,
  melted

1 egg

¼ tsp vanilla extract

(Pictured on page 172.) In trying to create the perfect healthy brownie, moisture was definitely an issue. Our secret ingredient? The sweet potato—our saving grace.

Preheat the oven to 350°F.

Sift the rice flour, cacao powder, and baking powder into a bowl.

Place the sweet potato purée, date syrup, melted butter, egg, and vanilla extract in another bowl and mix together well. Then stir in the dry ingredients.

Pour the brownie mixture into a rectangular cake pan lined with baking parchment and bake for 20–25 minutes, until set on top but gooey in the middle.

Cool in the pan, then cut into 8 pieces.

WHAT IS RAW CACAO POWDER?
This is one of the most amazing "superfoods." It's so rich in antioxidants, which help to make our systems strong to fight off any illnesses.

Poached Pears with Star Anise and Cashew Cream

serves 4

4 ripe firm pears, peeled,
    quartered, and cored

5 star anise

1½ tbsp agave syrup

1 cup raw cashews

½ tsp vanilla extract

NUTRITIONAL NUGGET
The seeds of star anise contain potent antibacterial and antiviral properties and have been used throughout Asia for thousands of years.

(Pictured on page 173.) A perfect quick and easy sweet fix and after-dinner treat, particularly for those who want to clear their palate after a meal.

Preheat the oven to 325°F.

Place the pear quarters in an ovenproof dish large enough to hold them without overlapping, add water to half cover the pears, then add the star anise and drizzle over 2 teaspoons of the agave syrup. Bake for about 25 minutes, or until tender.

Meanwhile, whiz the cashews with the vanilla extract and scant 1 cup of water in a blender until smooth and creamy. Transfer to a serving bowl.

When the pears are cooked, remove them from the dish with a slotted spoon and set aside. Pour half the cooking liquid into a pan with 2 of the star anise and the remaining agave syrup and place over high heat for about 5 minutes, stirring constantly, until the liquid becomes thick and syrupy.

Serve the pears with the syrup, cashew cream, and a little of the remaining cooking liquid.

Chocolate Superfood Ganache

serves 12–14

For the chocolate sauce

4 cups raw cacao powder

2 tsp ground cinnamon

3⅔ cups agave syrup

2 tsp Himalayan pink salt

2 tsp vanilla extract

½ cup coconut oil

For the ganache

1 quantity of Chocolate Sauce

3 tbsp maca powder

1 tbsp spirulina

1 tsp ground cinnamon

Scant ⅔ cup shelled raw hemp
   seeds

This is the most rich and indulgent recipe in the whole book. Enjoy with no guilt at all, as you deserve it—and anyway, it's full of superfoods!

To make the sauce, whiz the ingredients in a blender until smooth.

To make the ganache, whiz the chocolate sauce with the maca powder, spirulina, and ground cinnamon in a blender until smooth. Pour into an 8-in square baking pan or springform cake pan, lined with baking parchment, and sprinkle over the shelled hemp seeds.

Place the pan in the freezer for 20 minutes until the ganache is set, then cut into portions and enjoy.

NUTRITIONAL NUGGET
Hemp seeds are packed with the essential fatty acids omega-3 and omega-6 oils in one of the healthiest ratios around. What's more, these seeds are a rich source of the super-polyunsaturated fatty acids, notably gamma-linolenic acid.

WHAT IS RAW MACA POWDER?
Maca is a food the Incan gods considered an aphrodisiac. Some say this fantastic antioxidant helps to regulate hormones. Deliciously sweet, it's excellent in baking. It should be avoided by anyone with breast cancer as it has been known to have hormone-stimulating properties.

Lemon and Poppy Seed Almond Cake

serves 10

4 eggs

Scant ¼ cup honey

Generous ¾ cup vegan butter,
 plus extra for greasing

2 cups ground almonds

1 tsp baking powder

Finely grated zest and juice of
 3 small or 2 large lemons

2 tbsp poppy seeds

Melted raw chocolate, for
 topping (optional)

This is quite simply my favorite cake ever—it's so easy and quick to make. Just pop on a few candles and, hey presto, you have a perfect birthday cake.

Preheat the oven to 325°F.

Whisk the eggs and honey together in a bowl.

Mix the butter and ground almonds thoroughly in a separate bowl, then gradually stir in the egg mixture until smooth.

Add the baking powder and the lemon zest and juice and mix thoroughly, then stir in the poppy seeds.

Pour the mixture into a greased 8–10-in springform cake pan and bake for 30 minutes, until golden (cover the top with foil if it starts to brown too quickly). The cake is cooked when the top feels springy when you press it gently, or the tip of a sharp knife or skewer inserted into the center of the cake comes out clean.

Cool on a wire rack, then top with melted chocolate, if using.

TIPS

Some extra special tweaks:
- Omit the poppy seeds and use the finely grated zest of 2 small oranges instead of the lemons for an orange almond cake.
- Omit the poppy seeds, add ½ cup raw cacao powder and reduce the almonds to scant 1⅔ cups for a chocolatey one.

Tuck into these and make "sin" an emotion of the past. There is no sin in healthy food!

Coconut Flour Chocolate Mousse Cake

serves 10–12

Generous ¾ cup coconut flour

½ cup raw cacao powder, plus ½ tbsp for dusting

2 cups Hemp Milk (see page 57)

½ cup light olive oil non-dairy spread, plus extra for greasing

⅓ cup agave syrup

2 tbsp yacon syrup

2 tbsp almond butter

4 eggs

1 tsp vanilla extract

(Pictured on page 180.) This is a very dense, moist cake and is too amazing for words! Either make a thin "torte," as illustrated here, or bake in a smaller pan for a deeper, more luxurious-looking cake.

Preheat the oven to 300°F.

Sift the coconut flour and cacao powder into a bowl.

Place the hemp milk, non-dairy spread, syrups, almond butter, eggs, and vanilla extract in a blender and whiz for about 1 minute, until well blended (the mixture will be a little frothy on top). Gently fold the wet ingredients into the flour mixture until combined. The mixture will have quite a thick consistency.

Transfer the mixture to a lightly greased, base-lined springform cake pan (use a large, shallow pan for a thin, torte-like cake or a smaller, deeper pan for a thicker cake). Bake for 30–50 minutes, depending on the thickness. The thicker the cake, the longer it will need—check after 30 minutes by inserting a skewer into the center of the cake. If it comes out clean, then it is cooked. Otherwise, continue cooking, checking every 10 minutes. The cake will continue to set when cooling.

Leave to cool in the pan for 30 minutes, then transfer to a serving plate. Serve warm or cold, lightly dusted with cacao powder, with a scoop of one of our ice creams or sorbets (see pages 183–189).

WHAT IS YACON SYRUP?
This dark, thick caramel-like syrup is a sugar alternative. It's packed with fructo-oligosaccharides, which are sugars that aid digestion and which are absorbed slowly into the bloodstream, as well as being high in vitamins A, C, and E.

Lychee, Mango, and Basil Sorbet

serves 4–6

7 oz lychees, peeled and pitted

7 oz mango, chopped

1 tsp grated lime zest

2 tbsp lime juice

Scant ⅔ cup agave syrup

Scant 1 cup water

3 packed tbsp basil leaves

(Pictured on page 181.) This will blow the socks off any sorbet you have tried—you don't need heaps of sugar, as you'll see, to make this a wonderfully sweet fix.

Whiz all the ingredients in a blender until smooth.

Transfer the mixture to an ice-cream maker and freeze according to the manufacturer's instructions. Transfer to a freezer-proof container, cover, and freeze until firm.

If you don't have an ice-cream maker, transfer the mixture to a shallow freezer-proof dish and place in the freezer until it just starts to harden around the edges. Whisk vigorously with a fork to break up any ice crystals, then freeze until firm.

NUTRITIONAL NUGGET
Basil has abundant vitamin C and its essential oil is highly protective for the skin. This could explain why it is native to hot countries—nature will always provide what is needed, where it's needed.

Shepherd's Chocolate Ice Cream

serves 6–8

1⅓ cups goat's milk

5 oz xylitol

3 large egg yolks

Scant 2 cups sheep's yogurt

1 tsp vanilla extract

½ tsp vanilla powder

3 tbsp raw cacao powder

1 tbsp mesquite powder

2 tbsp raw cacao butter, melted

WHAT IS XYLITOL?
Xylitol has the lowest glycemic index (GI) of all the sugar alternatives. It's super-sweet but has a fresh minty undertone (why it's used in chewing gum) and is also rumored to be good for your teeth. It's great for baking!

We call it "shepherd's" ice cream because it's made with sheep's yogurt, which just makes it feel incredibly indulgent and creamy beyond belief. So, enjoy your chocolate ice cream—'cos you can!

Combine the goat's milk and 3½ oz of the xylitol in a heavy pan and bring to a simmer, stirring constantly, until the xylitol starts to dissolve.

Whisk the egg yolks with the remaining xylitol in a large, heatproof bowl until blended. Gradually add the hot milk mixture, whisking constantly, until blended. Return the mixture to the pan and cook, stirring constantly, over medium-low heat for about 3 minutes, or until the custard thickens slightly and coats the back of the spoon. Be careful not to let it boil. Remove from the heat and set aside to cool, stirring occasionally to make sure it doesn't split.

Meanwhile, combine the yogurt, vanilla extract, and vanilla powder in a large bowl. Gradually whisk the cooled custard into the yogurt mixture.

Stir the cacao powder and mesquite powder into the melted cacao butter and gently whisk into the custard mixture.

Transfer the mixture to an ice-cream maker and freeze according to the manufacturer's instructions. Transfer to a freezer-proof container, cover, and freeze until firm.

If you don't have an ice-cream maker, transfer the mixture to a shallow freezer-proof dish and place in the freezer until it just starts to harden around the edges. Whisk vigorously with a fork to break up any ice crystals, then freeze until firm.

Banana Toffee Crunch Ice Cream

serves 4–6

Scant 1 cup Almond Milk (see
   page 57)
7 oz xylitol
Scant 2 cups sheep's yogurt
¼ tsp xanthan gum
1½ tbsp agave syrup
1½ tsp lemon juice
2 bananas, chopped

For the toffee brittle
1 tsp coconut oil, melted
4 tbsp Brazil nut butter
1 tsp agave syrup
Generous ⅓ cup raw pecans,
   chopped
3 fresh dates, pitted and
   chopped
Pinch of Himalayan pink salt

This is toffee without the toffee. It's a little more complicated to make but is definitely worth having a go, and the end result is a match for any Italian ice cream.

To make the toffee brittle, stir all the ingredients together in a bowl, then spread onto a flat baking sheet, cover with plastic wrap, and freeze for about 40 minutes, until hard.

Combine the almond milk and xylitol in a pan and bring to a simmer, stirring constantly, until the xylitol starts to dissolve. Allow to cool, then gradually whisk into the yogurt in a bowl, adding the xanthan gum halfway through.

Stir in the agave syrup and lemon juice and finally add the bananas.

Transfer the mixture to an ice-cream maker and freeze according to the manufacturer's instructions. Transfer to a freezer-proof container, cover, and freeze until firm, adding the toffee brittle, broken into small pieces, once the ice cream is set but not too firm.

If you don't have an ice-cream maker, transfer the mixture to a shallow freezer-proof dish and place in the freezer until it just starts to harden around the edges. Whisk vigorously with a fork to break up any ice crystals, then freeze until firm.

Strawberry and Coconut Ice Cream

serves 4

2 cups strawberries
Scant 1 cup coconut cream
½ cup coconut water
2 tbsp agave syrup
¼ tsp vanilla powder
½ tsp xanthan gum
½ tsp lemon juice

Making ice cream doesn't have to be a tricky game—it takes a little patience, but this recipe is very easy and the chunks of strawberry give it such a great vibrancy.

Chop and gently crush generous ⅓ cup of the strawberries and set aside.

Whiz the remaining ingredients in a blender until smooth. Pour the mixture into a bowl and stir in the crushed strawberries. Transfer to an ice-cream maker and freeze according to the manufacturer's instructions. Put in a freezer-proof container, cover, and freeze until firm.

If you don't have an ice-cream maker, transfer the mixture to a shallow freezer-proof dish and place in the freezer until it just starts to harden around the edges. Whisk vigorously with a fork to break up any ice crystals, then freeze until firm.

This beautiful ice cream is so simple to make, with only four ingredients—and it's raw. Bonus!

Raw Blueberry Ice Cream

serves 4

⅔ cup raw cashews

Generous 1⅛ cups frozen blueberries

⅓ cup water

2 tbsp agave syrup

Whiz all the ingredients in a blender until smooth, then freeze in an ice-cream maker according to the manufacturer's instructions. Transfer to a freezer-proof container, cover, and freeze until firm.

If you don't have an ice-cream maker, transfer the mixture to a shallow freezer-proof dish and place in the freezer until it just starts to harden around the edges. Whisk vigorously with a fork to break up any ice crystals, then freeze until firm.

Index

Big Thank Yous from Tash and Vix

We would like to give a huge thank you to Jacqui Small for making the book happen and seeing our vision. To Lisa Linder, with her amazing photographic skills made our food look as utterly mouthwatering as it tastes. And to the book's whole team for their perseverance, patience and politeness. Thank you to Kelly (Mummy) for letting me steal (without knowing) most of her crockery and cutlery for the shoot! Big love to the British farmers and growers who have provided us with the most delicious produce for us to create with.

Tash says: I would like to send massive healthy love to Hayley North for being involved in this book. I'd like to thank all my friends for being such great guinea pigs, by making all the right noises at my dinners. My dad for sitting in the "cupboard" on Skype talking to me when I was cooking at home alone. The two wonderful fruit & veg stalls outside number 158 Portobello Road for their ever-tasty veg and letting us do our photo shoot. And a grateful hug to Joshi who introduced me to how amazing alkaline living can really be.

Vix says: To Robert Young, the pioneer of the alkaline approach who I had the good fortune to meet several years ago, and whose radiance and total focus inspired me. To my many clients who have given me feedback on the principles of the Cleanse and Lifestyle and shown me the results! And to Mother Nature herself who always provides us with what we need to sustain and nourish ourselves.

Directory of Food Suppliers

There are lots of suppliers online and you'll no doubt find your own favorites; here's a list to start you off.

Carrying over 400 products, **Bob's Red Mill Natural Foods** has almost every kind of flour (including gluten-free options) and whole grain you can imagine.
www.bobsredmill.com

Sold under the **Frontier Natural Products Co-op** and **Simply Organic** brands, this line of natural and organic products includes herbs, spices, and extracts.
www.frontiercoop.com

Herbs, Etc. offers a large variety of herbal products at www.herbsetc.com

Navitas Naturals specializes in 100 percent organic superfoods that are minimally processed, gluten-free, and kosher.
www.navitasnaturals.com

Pukka Herbs has stores all over the world including the US and Australia.
www.pukkaherbs.com

The go-to source for all things quinoa, **Quinoa Corporation** features certified organic ingredients.
www.quinoa.net

For fantastic supplements, check out **www.sunwarrior.com**

Trader Joe's has many all-natural and organic products.
www.traderjoes.com

You can find pretty much everything you need at **Whole Foods Market**.
www.wholefoodsmarket.com